# MOASSY, THE DOG

Jorge A. Livraga Rizzi

First Published in Spanish as *Möassy, el perro* in 1978
Translated from Spanish by Julian Scott
Redesigned for English edition by Neha Mehta

Published in 2023 by

NEW ACROPOLIS

New Acropolis Cultural Organization
Mumbai, India.

www.acropolis.org.in
info@acropolis.org.in



ISBN: 978-81-949468-6-1
Printed in India.

# MOASSY, THE DOG

Jorge A. Livraga Rizzi

# TABLE OF CONTENT

# FOREWORD

Moassy, the Dog is the last book by Argentinian-born philosopher Jorge Angel Livraga to be translated into English. Moassy is one of his more satirical, and perhaps autobiographical, works, albeit not less philosophical for being so. Satire has been used often by philosophers to pass their witty observations on the state of the world; Erasmus's "In Praise of Folly", and More's "Utopia" are some examples that come to mind. Through the journeys of Moassy, Livraga presents his penetrating and insightful observations on the state of the world of his times, which perhaps is not so different from ours, considering that human beings do not change so quickly. Interestingly, he never calls a country by its name, although the clever reader would be able to recognize each of the political entities, even if not all of them are still in existence today.

In his observations, Livraga transits easily from the most mundane to the most metaphysical, offering jewels of thought which invite the reader to additional reflection. Written in the early 70s of the last century, Moassy expresses sentiments and ideas that are not always in alignment with current beliefs, and therefore may be abrasive to some. But taken with a philosophical spirit, open to examine new and different ideas, one will benefit immensely from the somewhat controversial views presented in this little book, even if just to challenge one's existing opinions. Interestingly and sadly, many of the predictions made in this little book have already come to pass.

Reader, may you have a good journey. I hope you enjoy traveling together with Moassy. Even though Moassy does not consider himself very wise, perhaps we can all learn something from him...

Gilad Sommer
Director of New Acropolis Chicago

# BY WAY OF A PROLOGUE

Last night I felt cold. Although the thermometers recording the temperature of the air conditioning in my room indicated that it was warm, I felt cold... and a little bit anxious. No, it is not due to psychological reasons; I'm not very prone to psychological disorders, because I don't have much of a psyche. No; I think it's something more important... Perhaps the most important thing: I'm going to die. My unfailing instinct tells me so... Moreover, I have already lived for many years, too many for those of my race. I have tripled or quadrupled my normal lifespan, but now it's coming to an end.

This strange anxiety makes me want to drink water, to walk, to look through old photographs in search of friendly faces, to observe my own body with inexplicable curiosity; perhaps I want to say goodbye to it. Yes, now I am sure; I am going to die. And I cannot keep the terrible secret of my life for any longer.

I sit down in front of a typewriter; I put it on the floor to be more comfortable. Somehow, I go back to being a child again.

How strange! My breathing is not difficult, the air flows quickly into my lungs, but, as if it were stale, I cannot assimilate it and I feel an increasing sense of suffocation. I need to hurry; I need to write. Although I don't have much time, I feel that the hours are becoming longer for me and that I will be able to complete my task. At least I try to convince myself that I will. No one will be able to help me. When we are born and when we die, we are incredibly alone. And yet, I'm not afraid... and I don't know why I'm not afraid. Those of my race, in my situation, become sad and melancholic; that is not happening to me at all. If nothing awaits me after death, what is there to fear? Nothing matters any more... Or perhaps that's not true. If I could remain in front of the typewriter, and write, write... but I get up every now and again... as if I were looking for something or trying to escape... From what? From whom? I don't know.

My name is Moassy... sorry, Dr William Ferdinand Moassy.

This is the true story of my life. It is so incredible that I don't expect anyone to believe it. But truth is always unbelievable; there is nothing more believable than a lie. This little black wooden hut that awaits me on the horizon and is my death, does not disturb me, but reminds that I was born in another one, painted white, next to centuries-old pines and a new beehive, full of golden bees, drunk on honey and the music of their own wings. My mother had a beautiful red coat, my father... I don't know; I never knew my father. I had six brothers and sisters, all of them long dead, like my mother, like the bees.

Let me tell you...

CHAPTER ONE

# MY CHILDHOOD

In the depths of my time, like fragments of a boat that has sunk long ago, the memories of my childhood rise to the surface and disappear again. I see black water trying to submerge them; some of them, appearing for a brief moment, sink back forever. Others reappear again and again. I have to make an effort, in those brief intervals when they are visible, to retain something of their shapes, colours, sizes, natures...

From the darkest region, I draw the sensation of warmth and the rays of a very clear sun, peeping out, like the face of a mischievous child, between two mountain peaks. Then, enormous pine trees, many of them, of which I can only remember the powerful roots sinking into the earth towards the mysterious world of damp and deep darkness. And above, that other mystery of the heights, a mixture of blue, gold and white.

While my brothers and sisters were frolicking around, I lay still, gazing first at one infinity and then the other. And I would try to climb up the rough and ancient bark of trees, as if it were a vertical path, until I fell down, exhausted; and I would dig feverishly in the earth, but neither the earth nor the roots ever ended. My only possibility, like that of so many beings, was horizontal. The vertical, in one direction or another, was barred to me.

Among the fallen branches, the acorns, the pale trunks of poplars, my siblings and I used to play, following invisible labyrinths, getting lost and finding our way again amid short whimpers and equally short yelps of joy. At times, I would stop and gaze at the branches that had fallen from above: they came from the mystery of the heights, but, when they entered my horizontal dimension, they lost their green leaves and turned black. The earth I had dug up dried in the sun and became pale. They were both dead witnesses that could tell me little or nothing of those two infinities that obsessed me. Giving me a gentle push, my mother would urge me to run off again with my brothers and sisters. I discovered very early on that anyone who stops to reflect, is seen by others as sick. For that reason, I have always reflected on my own.

I was always different; I don't know if I was better, but I was different from others. As soon as I could look after myself, I started to go as far away as possible from the little white hut that had witnessed my birth, following the zigzagging flight of the golden bees. And then came the fear of loneliness and confusion; the only thing I knew was where the mystery of above and the mystery of below were; on this horizontal earth

I have always got lost. And I would laboriously return to my family, to my bowl of food, where the bones of other beings who, like me, had lived between two mysteries, were being bleached by the sun. When I understood that, I was horrified and would not taste food for several days. Then, hunger proved more powerful than the horror and pity: sad prophecy!

But then came a day, a day that dawned like so many others. The clouds shook off their sleep, stretched their moving arms and rose above the high valleys boxed in between mountains. The sun was pale; the air cold. But there was nothing to indicate that anything important was about to happen to me. And so it was that, after the washing that my mother subjected me to every morning, and a hurried breakfast among the palpitating bodies of my siblings, all anxious to go out and play, I left the white hut – though I didn't know it then – forever.

My departure was absurdly simple. I ran after the bees and couldn't find my way back again. At first, I was seized with despair and used all my instincts to discover the way back, but I couldn't. I told you: on the horizontal earth I have always got lost. But, when youth makes us restless and we begin to tire of the monotony of home, we soon forget our sorrows, so I kept running about and playing, and telling myself: "I'll worry about that later."

After the blazing hand of the sun had blessed the entire arc of the sky, it began to hide behind the mountains of the horizon, and the shadows, which during the day had kept timidly close to the objects, began to separate from them in order to begin their own cycle of races, running faster and faster. The stars stood out against the firmament which had now turned violet, and a cold wind, howling like a wolf, blew down from the mountains.

Still today, so many years later, I remember that first night of solitude with a shudder… Afterwards, one becomes accustomed to solitude, even if one continues to shudder. It's strange: there's a certain part of myself which is not afraid of solitude, and even enjoys it. I imagine that it must be that part which is always alone. But there are other facets of ourselves that see solitude in a dark light, and these are so afraid that sometimes with a part of our own body we squeeze and hold onto the other part, in a parody of company. Dissimilar natures that might lead us to deduce they have dissimilar destinies! But here I have already started philosophizing and I was in the middle of telling you about my childhood, and philosophy and childhood don't usually go together.

I made myself as comfortable as I could among the many feet of an immense tree and fell asleep; I don't know for how long. But I remember feeling the warmth of the sun and, at the same time, some hands lifting me up until I was looking at a face that was old and from which a snowy white beard hung, like an old rock. I whimpered and closed my eyes. I was no longer alone.

Shortly afterwards, a bowl of food and some words I didn't understand, but which I instinctively recognized as affectionate, restored in me a sense of peace. And they also made me aware that the little white hut where I was born, my mother and my playful siblings, had all been left behind. I was beginning a new cycle of my fantastic and incredible life.

My fingers have grown stiff on the keyboard of the typewriter, and I am intentionally delaying initiating you into my secret. I am only encouraged to keep going by the certainty that you won't believe me and that it is all true. If I were intelligent, I would find a way to express myself, but I'm not and I never was, and now I regret it, perhaps for the first time. Everything is piling up and becoming confused in my mind and I am even doubting that I will be able to finish writing this. But... courage! I must keep going. I will tell you once and for all: I, known today as Dr William Ferdinand Moassy, who has received so many honours from different countries around the world, and has sat on university boards and legislative bodies, I am... a dog.
Yes, laugh or be astonished, I am a dog. A dog who had a red coat, a wagging tail and a wet, calm nose. It is only my appearance that has been transformed, but I am a dog.

Now that you know my secret, I will continue trying to explain to you how I became transformed and how I made up for my lack of intelligence by the fact that human beings make so little use of their own.

CHAPTER TWO

# MY EDUCATION

My new master was a calm and gentle old man, extremely wise and kind-hearted. He was immensely rich and had some ancient noble title. He lived alone, in an old mansion crowned by a forest of chimney stacks, and was assisted by a veritable army of servants and secretaries.

After a restorative nap, I set about inspecting my new world. I had slept on a thick rug, in front of crackling fire which told the story of the thick logs from which it arose. I was surrounded by walls everywhere, although there was a lot of space between them. I could no longer see the two infinities of earth and sky, although I continued to be intuitively aware of them. This was a cosy and safe world; it was a refuge, in the widest and fullest sense of the word.

Fastening a collar around my neck, my benefactor took me

out for a walk through the immense gardens; but my childish apprehensions gradually faded under the warmth of the security of feeling so protected. Too much protection always dulls our subtle senses, but it can be useful at a certain time of our life.

Then came other days, weeks, months. Today, spurred on by the prospect of my approaching death, the memories of my childhood have returned, but at that time I had forgotten them. I lived just to please my benefactor, and he had lavished an unusual amount of care on me. Sometimes he would lift me up in his arms, despite the fact that my size was already more than respectable, and, letting me stand on my hind legs, observed me with a sarcastic and very sad look. Instinctively, I sensed that a strange pact was being forged between us. And I loved him as only a dog can love. By day I always walked beside him and by night I dreamt that we were running together through an infinite meadow, over emerald green grass and under a sky of lapis lazuli, while millions of golden bees did their work, carrying invisible pollen from always distant flowers to a hive that I could never clearly distinguish. In my dreams, I would see my benefactor and wake up gently, but with the sensation that there was something important in my dreams that I always forgot on waking.

My benefactor set my food before me with his own hands, and later I found out that it was not the usual kind of dog food, but a very complex mixture of conventional food and other types of his own invention. My physical development was, in truth, extraordinary; standing up on my hind legs, I would look my protector in the face, although I would immediately turn round and try to walk around his legs, distributing licks between his two thin and bony hands, which were adorned with several very old rings, set with stones of strange and changing reflections. I was slightly afraid of those rings and would have preferred him not to wear them. But I never saw him without them.

With time, my outdoor walks were restricted to those that I took in an enormous conservatory of multicoloured glass; and from there, without others seeing me, he led me to his private apartments, where only his most trusted servants, of Eastern origin, entered to clean the rooms in our absence.

With reprimands and rewards, he began teaching me to understand a few simple words; then he took me to his laboratory, where, after placing a kind of metal rod with a tangy flavour on my tongue, he made me reproduce some sounds that were unusual for me. By combining those sounds I began to formulate simple words, although my voice sounded horrible. Lying down between two enormous stone disks, I lay still, at his command, for several hours a day. When I got up, I saw that my red coat was gradually being left there, discoloured and pale. I began to feel cold, and thick blankets like horse rugs were provided for my protection, although I always found them uncomfortable.

I didn't know what my benefactor's intentions were, but I intuitively sensed that the treatment he was giving me was inappropriate for my race; something mysterious and terrible, which I feared, but at the same time longed to carry out. If that is what that exceptional man wanted me to be, that's what I would be. Apart from that, I felt pain for the immense sadness which he sometimes showed, and I had noticed that, when I performed my exercises correctly, that sadness disappeared. For me that was reward enough. His happiness was mine.

With infinite patience he taught me how to move the fingers of my paws under the strange red rays emitted by the lamps in his laboratory. As the years passed, these became finer, acquired extreme mobility and, modelled by his will, became similar in all respects to those of humans. In this way he modified the other parts of my body, even subjecting me to several plastic surgery procedures which left me without a tail... Although I still feel that I move it when I'm happy. I learnt to smile and not to cry as much as I would have liked; I began to be more and more similar to humans. But this transformation never became absolutely complete; although I learned to read and write, there are many things I still don't understand, and many others are impossible for me to express clearly.

My wise protector introduced me to the sciences and even to certain arts, but never to religion. Much later I studied the religious texts of the main forms of faith, ancient and modern; but I recognize once more the wisdom of that man, because I could never understand those subjects, and whenever I tried to raise the banners of my faith, a rain of fear and doubt came and flattened them on the ground.

With time I got used to wearing clothes. At first, I only wore them to protect myself from the cold, replacing the dog coats that used to slip off my body when I stood up. Little by little, from simple coverings I moved on to more elaborate garments and learnt to wash myself in the human manner.

After about ten years, I had taken on the appearance of a human being of a little over 30 years of age; my clothes and manners were correct and my general education quite broad, and I had mastered several languages, although with difficulty. But I knew nothing of the outside world. When I was ready, my protector, who was now very old, took me to see the nearest town, which was a small mountain village. It was my trial by fire; I was terrified that people would discover my canine nature, but my faulty pronunciation just made them take me for a foreigner or an eccentric. My powerful benefactor obtained for me, without difficulty, documentation that accredited me as the citizen of a far-off country and, pretending that I was a nephew of his, gave me his own forenames, but not his surname. He took this from an American Indian word; he called me Moassy.

At the beginning of winter, he began to decline. He would go to bed very early and not get up until midday. He became unsteady on his feet, and lawyers and various important people were constantly coming and going through his office, bringing and taking away documents. I later discovered that he had been transferring his immense fortune into my name, claiming that he had no family.

He had been born in a great country from which he had had to emigrate due to class struggles and persecutions. He had lost all his family in an assassination attempt. To overcome the pain, he had taken refuge for several years in a Tibetan monastery, until that monastery too was overtaken by the red waves of war and was destroyed... and, in some way, so was he. Driven to despair, he then took refuge in the enormous residence, surrounded by fortress-like walls.

For many years he worked in the immense cellar, setting up a complex secret laboratory, supplied with some of the most modern and expensive equipment in the world. When he found me, he used to repeat, his wish had been fulfilled, because, according to him, he had called me and had even caused me to be born for a single predetermined purpose. I never understood this, and I still don't completely believe it; but I loved him so much that, when I was in his presence, everything he said to me seemed to be the most absolute and irrefutable truth... In any case, I was never very concerned about the truth; even in that respect, I have always been similar to human beings.

I no longer kissed his now almost paralytic hands, always adorned with the mysterious rings, but I liked to lie at his feet and listen to him. He never prevented me from doing so, perhaps because he knew how important it was to me.
One warm and clear night, when I was at his side, on the thick rug that had been my first bed, he stroked my head and said to me:

'Moassy, tomorrow when the sun sets, I will die.'

My shocked silence allowed him to continue:

'Yes, I can no longer remain in this world; I have to make my way towards other, wider worlds. My work, which is you, is complete. You will inherit everything that is mine, apart from my laboratory, which will be blown up in a few hours' time… and a secret, which I will take with me.'

However strange it may seem, after the initial shock I didn't feel sad. Or perhaps I didn't completely understand his words, or I had already been expecting that ending for some time, so when it finally happened, I found it normal. But don't judge me too harshly; I continued to love him with all the strength of my being, and if I accepted his death without trying to take him away from his own destiny, it was because I saw that he was at peace with it, and almost happy. He continued:

'Moassy… I am going back… You will remain a little longer in this deceptive dimension, full of fantasy, passion, ignorance and pain. I ask you, innocent creature, to try to forgive me one day for what I have done to you, but through your existence you will prove a number of things…

'What things?' I interrupted him.

'No, Moassy… You have already learned all you could from me; now you must continue alone… No more words; I am not going to tell you anything more, and we will not say goodbye to each other either… We will look into each other's eyes, just like now, just like when I recognized you, asleep and shivering with cold at the foot of that enormous tree.'

We looked into each other's eyes for a long time; there were no tears and no more words… With a gentle whimper, I curled up at his feet and fell asleep, until a terrible explosion shook the floor beneath me. He did not move from his armchair. Far away, the staff of the mansion could be heard fighting the fire. Then, the sirens of the police cars and fire brigade. No one called at his office; no doubt his secretaries and lawyers were already prepared and had dealt with everything. He, my benefactor, gave no sign of having heard anything. I fell asleep again. When I awoke, the sun was already high in the sky and was filtering in through the ancient glass of the gothic windows in many colours. My benefactor remained asleep, although in his hands I noticed a little stick of charred wood and saw that the stones of his rings looked faded, as if they were tarnished.

I went out to inspect the damage, which had been limited to the underground laboratories, and attended to different matters concerning the running of my benefactor's businesses, which I had been representing with full powers for almost a year.

When the sun began to set, I cut about a hundred roses from the gardens with my own hands and went into his office with my offering. My protector was still sitting in the same armchair and in the same position, but now five concentric circles formed by little sticks of bamboo, or something similar, stuck into the parquet floor, were burning around him. However, only I had the keys to that wing of the building and I didn't understand how anyone could have entered... Who? I don't know either, but my instinct told me immediately that it had not been my benefactor, that there had been other beings in the room...

I was seized with a spine-chilling, instinctive and infinite fear. I threw open my arms, dropped the roses and ran whimpering towards the gardens, until I collapsed with exhaustion by the cars parked in the garage. The mechanic looked at me in surprise, but didn't ask me anything.

An hour later I took an internal telephone call; one of my benefactor's valets informed me that he had been found dead in his bed.

How had he got there if he had already seemed to be dead when I left him? I don't know, I didn't want to know then and I still don't want to know now... There are some things that it is better not to know, especially if one is a dog.

There was a simple funeral.

I was alone now, but I didn't feel fear or sorrow; just a great, enormous tiredness.

CHAPTER THREE

# HOW I BEGAN TO MAKE MY WAY IN THE WORLD

Once the enormous fortune and list of contacts and influences I now had at my disposal had been established, I decided to leave everything in the hands of a management company and, with limited means, to make my own way towards a destiny which at that time was unknown to me and which I still don't understand... or perhaps I do.

I moved to a large city; I rented a simple and comfortable room and went out to look for work. The employment agency I went to, put me through a series of tests which I found childish. It was all about answering some simple questions and pushing some coloured little sticks through a maze as quickly as possible. 'Moassy,' I said to myself, 'remember when you were playing with your little brothers and sisters;' and everything turned out well. They also made me do some other silly exercise I can hardly remember, sitting at a desk with a mirror above it. All I can recall is that I solved it immediately by comparing it to the pond I used to look at myself in when I was a puppy. When they asked me about my political and religious ideas, I grunted something confused, which was vague enough to be interpreted as reasonable adherence to the generally accepted opinion. After many tests and filling out an infinite number of forms, I was finally accepted as a medical sales representative. A short course would complete my training.

I remember that, in my younger days, even though the human form that covered me made me look quite mature, all these requirements gave me a feeling of happiness, because I thought that the world of humans was well organized. If they required such tests for recommending remedies to doctors who should already know about them, what would they not require for qualifying as a professional; for raising a family; for, at the pinnacle of responsibility, governing a country...? Later I found out... but at that time I didn't know; and I thought that the archetype of culture and refinement that my protector had been for me was the common standard for all human beings.

I found the job extremely enjoyable from the outset. The doctors I visited all seemed to be very knowledgeable and serious. All I had to do was read them the brochure that came with the medicines and they would grunt their approval, giving me the impression that they already knew all about them and clearly understood their advantages and disadvantages. Not one of them ever asked me a question. They all seemed to know everything. At that time, I found the world of humans delightful.

I made so much progress that I was put in charge of a large team of sales representatives, and with the free time I now had available, I decided to start a university course, since I already had secondary qualifications from the time I had been with my benefactor. The only thing I found intimidating was the prospect of the difficult tests I would have to pass in order to be admitted to a "higher education institution". But the reality, as happened so many times, proved to be different to what I had imagined.

The qualifying entry tests were little more than a formality; and once I was enrolled as a student, as long as I repeated what I was taught by each of the lecturers, I was able to complete my course quickly. My good memory, which had been highly trained, allowed me to obtain the highest marks, and my natural instinct always led me to track down the latest short summaries that were indispensable for the exams.

Whenever a fellow student showed me the posters that had been put up on the walls by political activists, I just made an indiscriminate sound, as I didn't understand them, and this was enough for me to become more and more popular, because everyone thought – now I know – that I was agreeing with them.

The word "everyone" is a way of referring to the active minority in the faculty. The fact is that most people, the vast majority, almost all the students, limited themselves to studying when they could, while the strikes and forced closures dictated by their "representatives" gave them some breathing space and even inspiration. Those of you who are younger may not believe me, but until just a few years ago, that higher education institution offered little in the way of education and was really a dumping ground for all the social misfits and guerrillas in the area. In this way, I got to know many people who idealized the poor, but drove luxury cars; who had liberated themselves from the taboo of not speaking about sex, but had adopted the taboo of not speaking about the soul, God, honour, or concord.

Perhaps because I was a dog, I didn't understand such ambiguities. If we extol those who have thin coats of fur and get rid of those who still have thick ones, the sum of the first will produce generations who have increasingly less protection; and will *cold,* even when shared by all, be less cold for each individual?

But I kept my thoughts to myself, because as I am a mere dog, a simple product of nature, I didn't dare to disagree with those who, sitting at a table in a café, solved the eternal problems of humanity in a couple of hours. In this way, I preferred to remain silent or grunt ambiguously in the face of their theorizing. This meant that nothing interfered with my performance in my exams, and within a few years I was awarded a doctorate in a couple of disciplines.

One of my theses dealt with the subject of "monoculture". I had observed that students were introduced, from the first year onwards, to a form of unilateral thinking based on myths and legends, on abstractions which tried to idealize something that was not idealizable. History, religion, philosophy and art were always studied from the "a priori" point of view of certain affirmations which, by being repeated, came to resemble truths for the inexperienced young people. Thus, their "awareness" was "raised", and the dwarfocracy[1] diminished in their eyes all the great human beings and heroes who have ever existed in the world. The addition, subtraction, multiplication and division of all this meant that an Alexander was seen as nothing more than a lucky drunk; Jesus Christ, an unlucky anarchist; Saint Teresa of Avila, a sexually frustrated woman; and Gandhi, a champion of guerrilla warfare. All of this is a phenomenal historical absurdity and a negation of the most elemental principles of logic, but with my dog-like astuteness, I discovered that the more nonsense I talked, the more I was appreciated, and the higher I threw my mud, the greater the glory I achieved for myself.

In this way, and against my convictions, out of respect for the opinions in fashion amongst human beings and out of my own interest in fully understanding this whole enigma which presented me with so many violations of reason, I extolled a politicizing monoculture: I gave resounding and pompous names to mob rule, and I highlighted every true or untrue defect I could attribute to any heads that rose above the historical horizontality of nations. My thesis won a prize; I graduated and was awarded my PhD.

I still vividly remember that day. After the ceremony in which the diplomas and prizes were awarded, clothed in a solemnity which, given the circumstances and the principles on which the university claimed to be based, was out of place, I retired

---

1 Translator's note: a term coined by the author referring to a system where everything is reduced to the lowest common denominator.

to my simple room, took off all my clothes and, curling up on the floor, tried to go back to being a dog like any other. So ashamed was I of being similar to human beings.

I discovered that my childhood as a dog, spent with my affectionate mother and my playful and healthy brothers and sisters, framed by mountains and forests, and stimulated by the simple joy of being alive, had been better than that which was offered to a human child, condemned from birth to live trapped between arguments and crucified on a cross of fear, held down by the headless nails of violence.

I found that my love and loyalty for my protector and master were feelings that were no longer in use, rusted by the viscous humidity of the armpits of the dwarfocracy. To love a teacher, a prophet, a natural leader, had become stupidity and sentimentality. Number, in terms of quantity, had displaced ideas, in terms of quality. The piling up of many things in confusion, like a mass of worms, to be rolled downhill towards the swamp of a diluvial world of primitive animal life, when not even domestic animals had appeared, that was the ideal; that was liberation; that was the goal; that was the only destiny that human beings could imagine, and which, by law of affinity, they were creating...

I still shudder when I think of that day... How I would have loved to be able to howl all my pain as I used to, and to silence this transplanted mind that made me see so many horrors! I no longer remember whether I remained in that state for one day or several. I do remember, though, that I did not eat for a long time, which is the way we dogs express our unhappiness, because, in our simplicity, happiness, well-being and health are synonymous.

Once I had recovered, I decided to return to my protector's mansion, which was now mine. I needed to think, to rest, to cry a lot. I needed to visit his tomb and ask him things. He had told me, on one occasion, that in the grave there is nothing but dross, and that the fire of the soul, with the best part of itself, rises up towards other dimensions. But I know nothing of that; I only know that I love him as I always did, that I need him more than ever. I feel this today, as I write, and I felt it at that moment. I believe that, in what human beings call "spiritual" matters, I have not made any progress at all. It is so easy to accumulate wealth and honours, and so difficult to obtain a single drop of that imperishable draught of right knowledge, of certain faith, of final gnosis!

Ah! If only I could manage to break down that wall of fog that separates me from my master and protector, how many questions I would ask him...! Or perhaps I wouldn't; perhaps I would simply lie down at his feet.

CHAPTER FOUR

# CROSSROADS

It's surprising how lucid one becomes in the final hours of life. Despite the fact that my body feels increasingly clumsy and unwell, my memory is growing stronger. Yes, it is not the memory that remembers; rather, it is memories that create our memory, another victim of that implacable survival instinct that affects all things and beings. The shadows of past things refuse to disappear and take refuge in some part of ourselves, that part which we call memory.

But my canine intuition, which I have never lost, tells me that those memories were not born when the events that apparently gave rise to them in the mechanism of consciousness came to an end, but that they come from the infinite future and go to the infinite past through us. Yes, they pass through us, they wound us and leave... Ah, the cuneiform mystery of the scars of the soul! A lost language for the many, but not a non-existent one. I, a simple dog who had a red coat, but later also had a master, a protector, a king, I know this... today better than ever. But I have interrupted my story, and you are interested in my story, not in me... That is also something I have learnt.

I have entitled this chapter *Crossroads* because, at that time, I really didn't know what to do with myself and with the divine and diabolical responsibility that I held in my hands.

There is something I haven't made sufficiently clear to you: my appearance never became completely human, but much later I understood that human beings had forgotten to look into each other's eyes, to look at each other directly in the face; and so, as no one was ever interested in that, I was never discovered. But at that time, I was afraid that I would be; my qualifications and wealth were not enough to free me from that unsettling fear. Fear is like a dog's coat: it always accompanies us, we lose it periodically, it grows back again and only leaves us in extreme old age, and even then, not completely. So, what should I do? When we dogs have doubts, we start walking; and that's what I did. I embarked on a long series of journeys, without any fixed course, without a destination in this horizontal world, but always trying to catch a glimpse of the two infinities.

To get the most out of my travels, prior to my departure, I spent a year studying the enormous private library of my master and protector. I visited his tomb. I imagined my own. I meditated through the long nights and read dozens of volumes. I listened to music, admired works of art and, as evening fell, I sought refuge in the museum of the mansion, sitting in the half-light, watching the brightness and the colours of the Egyptian pieces changing with each step of the sun and each jump of the shadows, until, finally, everything faded into an enigmatic darkness crossed only by strange phosphorescent forms, creaking sounds that would have been inaudible to those who did not have the hearing of a dog, and cold little winds that made the now non-existent hairs on my back stand up on end. Then I would get up from my armchair and play the mansion's electronic organ so loudly that its very foundations, nestling in the depths of the earth, trembled as I did...

My eccentricities did not alarm my secretaries or my household staff. I discovered very early on that the only thing that concerns most human beings is their food and, their material comfort. As long as they have that in abundance, nothing alarms them, regardless of what they see and hear. This disheartened me, but at the same time, on the strictly personal level, it gave me confidence. Having sufficient means, no one would pay attention to me, only to my financial resources.

I had already decided to travel, but how and with what apparent aim? I decided, after much consideration and after discussing the matter with my technical, legal and financial advisers, to buy a large ship and obtain some scientific-cultural mission, both of which were easy for me to do.

In about two months, everything was ready for my departure. My vessel, now fitted out like a gigantic yacht, had a displacement of 7,000 tons and a library of carefully selected books, an electronic organ, a couple of helicopters, some works of art, a catering service, and everything that can turn a boat into a first-class floating hotel. A group of intellectuals would accompany me, and another very large group of well-paid assistants. In addition, of course, to the seamen and ship's officers.

But I had a problem: what would I call the ship? If I gave it the name of my master and protector, I would be accused of being a family-obsessed egomaniac; if I used that of an ancient sage, it would be rejected by the younger generation; if I gave it the name of a well-known young person, it would not be approved of by the powerful. How much I deliberated! I even thought of calling it Europe, but when I arrived in America, Asia or Africa, the inhabitants of those continents, with their localisms, would feel a subconscious rejection towards it. And the same would happen the other way around, because human imbecility owns the passports of all nations and easily crosses all borders without many checks or formalities. Stupidity has always had the greatest freedom to travel across the world. I would look, then, for a solution stupid enough to satisfy everyone.

I took four letters at random and had them placed, in enormous sizes, on the bow and stern of my ship. They were a D, an R, an O and a C. I don't know why I chose them, but you will see that I chose well, which is the prerogative of those who don't think, like dogs. They were mounted on a system of openings which allowed their order to be changed in different combinations, according to my wishes... or rather, according to the wishes of human beings, who have always known more about this than me.

I settled my affairs and departed. I felt confident, but not happy.

CHAPTER FIVE

# MY FIRST JOURNEY

After a long sea crossing, rather too calm for my liking, the captain, an extraordinarily competent man, informed me that in a few hours' time we would be arriving at our first port of destination, in an old country with strong beliefs in religious matters. I nodded and withdrew to my apartments to revise my knowledge of the nation I would be visiting for the first time, when a question took me by the ear, as we dogs say, and I went up to the bridge.

A number of officers were drinking coffee, while the one on duty, who was sitting in his chair steering the yacht, looked up at the horizon, and then down at the many little lights that lit up a horseshoe shaped panel surrounding him. The captain was also there, so I called him aside and asked him in what order he had placed the four letters which were supposed to be the initials of the name of the boat. Smiling, he answered that the first was R, followed by D, then O and finally C. Without waiting for my reply, he explained:

'Doctor, your ship is now called: *Restored Divine Omnipotent City*; I have already radioed this name when requesting permission to enter territorial waters, and the relevant documentation has just been printed out on the on-board printer. Within an hour a helicopter will take off from the deck with our representatives to finalize the bureaucratic details.'

I was left speechless and, in view of the undisguised laughter of the captain and the complicit silence of the other officers, I rushed to the stern and, leaning over as far as I could, read the small explanatory sign that was hanging under the enormous aluminium letters which, effectively, were in the order he had announced: R, D, O, and C. You may be wondering why I was so astonished, when I had come up with this Machiavellian idea myself. The fact is that we accept many things in our fantasy and believe them to be true, but when we see them objectified in this impacting and material world, we are surprised, as if they were not our own children... Or perhaps it is precisely because they are.

I watched the helicopter take off with my ten representatives, and once again my nose quivered and I breathed heavily. On its flank, where those aircraft usually have their name or identification, an enormous letter R stood out, although I was not able to ascertain its meaning, because it was not accompanied by the other three letters. I called the ingenious captain again and asked him what it meant. He answered that if I had better eyesight, I would have been able to read the small sign below it that spelt it out. It stood for: *Rosary*. Already irritated by the excessive ingenuity of my captain – because ingenuity, if it is someone else's, is always annoying – I ordered him to make sure that, whichever country we would go to, the helicopter announcing my arrival would always be the same one and the letter R should not be changed, after which I looked at him with an undisguised air of triumph. Without waiting for any reaction on his ice-cold face, I quickly made my way down to my private cabins.

From that day onwards a strange relationship began between the old officer and me; I think we detested each other, but at the same time there was a mutual admiration. For me, he was the antithesis of my deceased protector and master. When I was with him, I felt insecure, and what I learned from him always had a touch of evil about it. However, I never thought of dismissing him, and he didn't leave me either. Sometimes, because evil is a mere absence of good, it sucks us in like a vacuum pump and throws us against one another, sticking us together, merging us into one mass, as if we were squashed together in a dark ditch where there is no air of truth, with no hope other than hope itself.

Suitably dressed, surrounded by the cluster of intellectuals and well known personalities who formed my entourage, I met those who were to escort us in the main reception room of the boat and we disembarked. A few metres further on, a crowd of several thousand people were chanting slogans of some kind. The open hands of the placards moved backwards and forwards in an impulsive movement, as if they were going to throw the stones of their words scrawled in black at me.

The bells of hundreds of churches rang out, frightening the swallows into flight.

The spectacle was beautiful, but sad, and had a tragic air about it. After the official greetings, the playing of the national anthem and some other pleasant formalities, I walked through the middle of the cordoned-off crowd, in the direction of the official cars waiting some way off. Then I saw those who were waving their placards close up. They were very young, and not very clean. I stopped in front of a particularly aggressive group, who were shouting at the top of their voices, trying to get me to understand whatever it was they were shouting. I understood it: they were protesting against the gag of silence to which they were subjected. They were clamouring for freedom and the right to protest. I raised my arms, let out a short and very loud shout and continued on my way. After a moment's hesitation, the mass of young people started to cheer me and, shortly afterwards, withdrew in peace. I got into the black car, but I was not at peace.

The visits and celebrations lasted for several days. The people were genuinely religious, but, as they did not receive any deep instruction in those theological mysteries, there were many who followed them out of mere formalism, and even the priests, except for very honourable exceptions, had exchanged their spiritual exercises for routine prayers which they said mechanically, with hearts that were too dry and tongues that were too moist... Furthermore, topics concerning the soul and God, which ought to have been talked about in the churches, were being replaced by speeches about contraceptives, sociology and economics. I found it amusing to imagine religion being taught by doctors, sociologists and economists. This thought – I remember it vividly – comforted me, because if a priest could play the role of a sociologist and a politician could act as a saviour of souls, a dog could easily pass himself off as a man.

At one of the official banquets that were given in my honour – the second one, if I remember rightly – the officials besieged me with questions; the questions bit me here and there without giving me time to respond to one, before another claimed my attention. Those people had a problem, and a very serious one at that. Their political-social system was based on traditional structures in which the religious element was fundamental; but in those times, the younger citizens were abandoning the old forms or were reluctant to observe them wholeheartedly. In view of this, those who exercised the always crucial function of government had found no better response than to modify their own attitudes, in what they called "adapting to the times", using tactics which, according to them, had a hidden aim.

Intrigued by this, because perhaps due to my canine nature I did not understand it, and also slightly embarassed by the looks of mutual understanding and confident smiles that were being exchanged by all the humans present, including those accompanying me, I asked what this saving tactic might be. The explanation was not long in coming, and I had to recognize that it was simple and clear. It consisted in giving in to whatever the young masses demanded; if they preferred to talk about sex in the churches, sex was what would be spoken about; if they wanted to turn the universities into more or less disguised political committees, they would let them have their disguises; if, through pornographic publications, they wanted to transform woman into a mere dehumanized symbol of carnal pleasure, they would allow it; and if, finally, distinguished historical figures were to be replaced by fashionable bandits, with their brains and berets tilted to one side, no one would oppose it. In this way – they affirmed – through the experience of these fallacies, young people would become aware of their errors and would return by themselves to the most healthy customs and right thoughts.

After this explanation, all the humans laughed and once again exchanged shrewd looks and signs of understanding. But I remained silent and imperceptibly lowered my ears, while at the same time bowing my head, which is the pensive attitude of dogs. I quickly thought that if a puppy, due to inexperience and driven by its playful nature, inadvertently runs into a bog, its elders, when they see that it is sinking further and further in, even if it continues to bark happily, will go and rescue it as soon as possible, because once it reaches the quicksand, it will inevitably go under. All dogs know this: if a puppy runs into a marsh, the further it goes in, the dirtier it will come out, and if it goes in too far, it will never get out at all, because it will be swallowed by the quicksand which is the hidden heart of the marsh. In this way, I thought that if young humans were not looked after or guided by the more experienced ones, directing their future steps along firm paths, they would sink further and further into the mud, until the central morass of all that pseudo-freedom, which is atheism and anarchy, devoured them.

I expressed these thoughts in words that I can no longer remember, but was immediately interrupted by the thunderous laughter of everyone present. Once the laughter had died down, I heard comments such as: "What an excellent joke, Doctor! You have a fine sense of humour!" "To say that the liberation from customs and their democratization only makes the immoralities of the few available to the many! Write it down, Doctor, you are a consummate humourist!" And: "Dr Moassy affirms that the process is exponential and that it inexorably ends in anarchy and the destruction of society if it is not stopped in time... If it were not a joke, I would think he doesn't realize that this whole parody of change has been engineered by ourselves to keep the young people entertained, and that when we see a danger, we will reverse the process and everyone will be saved! Furthermore, as I'm sure he's aware, if a young person doesn't have these outlets, he will start to reflect and demand that the older generations adopt a monastic and inhuman attitude, which we are not in a position to offer... After all, we're not made of stone... and nor are the young people!"

I don't want to bore you with my memories, so I'm not going to repeat to you all the nonsense that assaulted my ears for the next half hour. Finally, raising my glass, I shouted in my discordant voice: "Let's drink to that." And everyone drank, although I never clarified what I was proposing as a toast; but each of them believed that it was their own idea, and this enabled me to get up from that table amidst applause and ovations.

A week later, I departed. A crowd of intentionally dishevelled young people, their expensive clothes deliberately stonewashed to give them a more worn-out look, began, as an act of protest, to urinate in the sea next to my boat. The government representatives who had come to see me off were laughing their heads off at the scene. From far away, at the back, a priest made a sign in the air and blessed us all. I bowed several times, my entourage did the same; from the shore, as our ship set sail, a clamorous ovation bid us farewell.

While the captain ordered the letters that abbreviated the variable name of my boat to be changed again, and everyone laughed, I took refuge in my cabin and did not answer the many calls on the internal telephone, because I did not want them to discover by my high-pitched voice that I was crying... Of course – you will say – as I was surrounded by humans rather than dogs, no one would have noticed that kind of crying; but on that evening I was not sure that I was surrounded by humans. And that doubt, I now confess, as I sense that I'm dying, never left me.

CHAPTER SIX

# MY SECOND JOURNEY

Well, I'm not really referring to a second journey, but to the same one. But when I remember it, for some strange psychological reason, I see each adventure, in each country, as different journeys. As that's how I feel it, that's how I'm writing about it. Even at the moment of death we should avoid lying... or are we always lying, even when we believe we are telling the truth? Or rather, are we always telling the truth in some form and manner, even when we are lying? If we take the universe as the reality, we will affirm the former; if God, the latter... But philosophical abstraction is always dangerous, because it allows us to justify ourselves and to justify others, whatever the position we assume. Virtue and reason do not always walk arm in arm, and truth always walks alone.

I remember clearly the special psychological atmosphere that developed as we approached the territorial waters of the next country we were to visit. The one we had left behind, in spite of its sanctimoniousness and difficulties, had not lost an old, but not worn-out sense of respect for the individual and for sacred and permanent things. The upheavals of its youth were just a passing phase, and as they grew older, they left as a legacy for the younger generation the fashion of a formal but inauthentic rebellion.

Everyone knew, at heart, that the cycles of history laugh at changes, and that what was in the beginning, is and always will be; that changing the labels of the packaging does not seriously affect the contents. They had upheld in my presence a formal religious absolutism, based on the duty of children to follow the religion of their parents in every detail; but when I reminded them that twenty centuries ago their ancestors had upheld other forms, and that those who had rebelled, on that previous occasion, in order to give birth to a new form of religion, had denied the principles of the old one, they had responded with some confused reasonings, which nevertheless expressed the inner conviction that the change had been more in name than in spirit. Even old images of gods, dressed up in modern clothes, were erected on new altars, accompanied by an irrepressible popular veneration.

But now we would be confronting a society that had uprooted itself from its own history and was as impressive as an arm that moves the fingers of its hands, while being cut off from its torso. Its physical strength was enormous, and an unnaturally materialistic outlook had become the obsessive sorcery of those humanoids who, without parents and without a God, had the untiring force of a machine.

Although, at least in my presence, no one mentioned it, I felt that they were afraid. We dogs can smell the fear of men and usually amuse ourselves at their expense. I admit it: day after day at the officers' table, I intentionally instigated conversations about the country we were about to visit and about the bloody and catastrophic revolution that had given birth to the "zombie" of its new form. The historians in my entourage tried to reflect on the driving forces of those changes and to predict new developments. The writers justified. The sociologists interpreted. The military people frowned, pretending to understand. But, beyond the professorial appearance I displayed to them, Moassy, the dog, smelt their biological and atavistic fear and bit the heels of their arguments, forcing them to run in another direction, different from the zigzagging movement that panic was making them adopt. And each time they escaped from me, I goaded them with the same topic over and over again, until the smell of fear revolted me and I went down to my quarters and locked myself in again, taking off my clothes and lying curled up on the rug, without thinking or doing anything apart from whimpering very occasionally, snuffling and shaking my mutated ears. We dogs can spend a very long time like this without doing anything else. It is our form of meditation and an expression of our weariness at having to live in a world dominated by human beings.

As my isolation, and the food that was returned to the hands of the waiters almost untouched, might alarm my fellow adventurers more than necessary, I decided one day to go up on deck and make cheerful conversation with everyone. The captain did not take long to approach me, with his indelible but almost imperceptible smile. To my unspoken question, he answered:

'Dr Moassy, your ship now has a new name...'

As I remained silent, looking at the sea, he continued:

'It is now called *Definitive Communist Revolutionary Order*.'

I would have liked not to show my surprise, but that man exceeded my highly developed self-control, and I couldn't help straightening up with indignation, and thus becoming the victim of his mocking laugh. Once again, he had managed to arrange the initial letters in the most suitable way.

The noise of the helicopter taking off, carrying the new documentation and my representatives, made me turn round quickly, but I could only make out the letter R on its side. Once again the captain anticipated my question and, in a complicit tone, said quietly:

'It's now called *Revolution*.'

I looked back at the sea again and was left alone. My ears were now assailed by the screeching laughter of the seagulls. I went down to my quarters with a nagging question in my mind: was Moassy laughing at the world or was the world laughing at Moassy? From the depths of myself, a voice, which sounded like that of my old master and teacher, answered: what does it matter?

I think I felt cold... Or maybe I am feeling cold now and I am associating my memories with this fleeting present which is falling towards death like a stone falling towards the bottom of a well. But let us continue with the story; memories, like hurried nocturnal visitors, tend to walk away from our door if we don't open it quickly and, lost in the night of forgetfulness, who can catch up with them? Memories wander in oblivion like muffled up passers-by in the fog; sometimes we lose sight of them, but they never disappear; they are always there, in some part of time.

We entered a large port where about a hundred cargo vessels were loading and unloading many different products, from supersonic aircraft to fishmeal. The smell was, in general, unpleasant, and the weather bleak; but the members of the committee that boarded our ship, from two lead-coloured launches, seemed respectably dressed, smiling, with well well-fed bodies and round faces. Contrary to what my officers had anticipated, no extraordinary security measures were in evidence. Everything seemed to have been organized with a lot of effort and good faith.

When we walked down the gangway, only a tiny reception committee was waiting for us. Some photographers took their pictures, but no one asked us any questions. My canine instinct told me that these people had no great desire to meet other people, disillusioned, perhaps, by an excessive self-analysis.

Although the officials were evidently aware of my boat's peculiarity of changing its name without altering its initials, they seemed flattered and praised its name with open smiles. As always, whenever I don't know what to say, I just grunted, which they took as the most gracious of comments because they all laughed loudly together. Then, for my "personal safety", they ushered me into a rather small black car, which was preceded and followed by several similar ones, and we drove through the streets of a surprisingly traditional city, populated by people who were surprisingly dressed in the old manner.

I perceived that world as being held in place by pegs that forced it to repeat itself day after day without much variation. They put me up in a hotel from the last century, in a set of rooms that had a faded luxury and reminded me of a Rococo museum. Everything seemed to have been well planned in advance, and my fellow travellers were also lodged in similar apartments. On large formal cards I was invited to a dinner that would be held in my honour that evening in the same hotel. Although no one ever stopped smiling, I never felt comfortable among them, because within a few minutes we had run out of topics of conversation, and were reduced to empty words of Victorian conventionality.

In the evening, my secretaries showed me the local newspapers, which reported on my arrival and on speeches that had never been made; the only genuine things were the photographs, but the reports were so ambiguous and innocuous that I had not the slightest cause for complaint or reason to protest about them. They were written in terms of a hollow diplomacy which I myself would most probably have used if I had been forced to do so by the circumstances.

Having inherited a noble title and so much wealth, I had expected a negative emphasis to be placed on that; but I found nothing of the kind. There came to my memory the words of the greatest leader this vast country had had during the Second World War: "A diplomat's words should bear no relation to action... Sincere diplomacy is no more possible than dry water or wooden iron." Without anyone noticing, I kept my ears imperceptibly pricked up, which is how we dogs reveal that ambiguous sensation between fear and attention.

I remember very little of the dinner; I was terribly bored by the long speeches at the end. Interminable. Numerous officials and hierarchs made great efforts to prove the efficiency of their respective projects, by reeling off statistics and technical data. They showed me their machines, but not their humanity. They highlighted the fact that their space rockets had left the Earth to travel millions of kilometres, but no one told me which planet had a human being on it. In response to my questions about why the stars moved, they were brilliant at explaining the latest mechanical theories, but I always asked them, at the end of their learned expositions: Why? For what purpose? With what aim? And my questions were always followed by the never-ending circle of other mechanical effects that were the causes of the ones that followed. Everything took place in the horizontal world... None of them could give me any explanation for the two infinities that obsessed me then and still obsess me now... "Above" and "below" were meaningless words for the technocrats and political commissars. Among human beings, class struggles; among stars, struggles between forces. But in reply to my "why?" and "for what purpose?", in response to my clumsy hands rising and falling as they pointed to the two infinities, they opened their arms horizontally, without seeing the bases or the pinnacle that I was suggesting to them and that my canine instinct never forgot.

After that, I don't know... I think everything faded into further conventionalities and the detailed reading of my itinerary. I don't remember anything that surprised me; I think I simply went to bed.

I have to fight against my tiredness and my indifference; sometimes I think it is not worth writing all this. A crowd of disconnected memories comes towards me... A hummingbird that has already died is pecking at a flower that withered a long time ago; waves that evaporated long ago, and became waves again dozens of times, break on beaches that have changed their forms; faces that have turned to dust still smile at me. The black hut becomes huge on the horizon like a windmill, but I don't know or I don't remember the colour of its flour or the shape of its bread. Curiosity drives me onward... Let's continue writing.

Without much ceremony, but surrounded by a large number of dignitaries, we boarded an enormous aeroplane that took us on a direct flight to the giant's head. Apart from a few modern and monotonous areas, where hundreds of square and soulless buildings were packed together like shoeboxes, the centre was adorned with beautiful parks and artistic buildings, and ancient towers topped by rounded and gleaming roofs, battlements and polychrome walls, spoke of an ancient splendour. Their interiors displayed the electronic brightness of a cybernetics that had grown fat by devouring dreams. The people, who had to work hard for a living, had frugal habits but were cheerful in their private lives, although in public they all displayed a strange apathy and indifference. Only the most rural – and probably the healthiest – people still had the spirit of an innocent camaraderie.

Unlike what happened to me on my arrival, and in spite of the extreme caution of my statements, and the moderate and efficient behaviour of my entourage, the welcome we received in the great capital was cold and extremely official. We were assigned to a modern, hard-looking hotel, as pale as a corpse. By the excessive number of attendants and other hotel staff we could tell that we were being closely watched. I was never able to go out for a walk in the street on my own; official etiquette always ensured that I was accompanied by several interpreters and guides, even though I had repeatedly made clear to them that I had a perfect command of the language of the country and could not get lost.

As the days passed by monotonously, I thought it was time to leave.

Before doing so I visited the impressive mausoleum of the greatest hero of that revolution which had uprooted this enormous country from its historical ancestors, and had turned it into the seedbed of universal dialectical materialism. In a glass coffin lay the body of one who had been a brilliant contradiction, a dwarf-like titan. Afflicted by a stammer, his passion led him to become a great orator; theoretical and intellectual, his fortune had turned him into the very image of the most pragmatic political action. Of bourgeois customs, a good husband, attached to the upbringing he had received in the almost noble family into which he had been born, he nevertheless promoted an anti-bourgeois ideology, free love and a demented hatred towards the very world that had given him birth. Some of his carefully selected phrases surrounded him like a halo of glory, and his moving figure expressed dedication to ideals and uprightness. Although, at that moment, there came to my simple mutated dog's mind one of his favourite expressions: "Pacts, agreements between men, are like pie crust: they are made to be broken."

As I was leaving, I was surprised to see an enormously long queue of people who were going to pay religious homage to one who reaffirmed that religion is the opium of the people. I felt happy when I left that place, and if I had still had my tail, I would definitely have wagged it under my trousers; I limited myself to shaking my ears and panting with satisfaction as I felt warmed by the sun that was filtering through the frozen air. Once more I thought of my two infinities and of the person whom I had seen lying there, so horizontal...

I can no longer remember what other things I did until the same large aeroplane took me to the port where my ship remained at anchor. But I do vividly remember the conversation I had, in the reception room, with a number of ideologists who had come to see me off.

Until that moment, both parties had avoided any topics that might have given rise to conflicts; but, on that last day, the mask of diplomacy slipped, and allowed a glimpse of the hidden face that was behind us all.

Sitting on two comfortable sofas, we and they came together in the pleasant surroundings of my boat, where Roman amphoras, Greek hydras, Egyptian images and horses from the Tang dynasty appeared here and there; unfortunately, I cannot say it was a "meeting of minds". Now the abyss between us was in plain sight and there was no bridge between the two sides. The dialogue which should have developed quickly turned into an exchange of fire that soon put an end to my patience, although theirs seemed infinite.

I remember the first question and my first answer, both of which, I recognize, were brutal:

'Doctor, how can you live surrounded by so many marble statues, while there are human beings in the world who are dying of hunger?'

'People, gentlemen, don't eat marble or ceramics. People are nourished by ideals, they drink faith, they wear clothes woven with concord...'

'But what about bread and blankets?'

'Bread and blankets are indispensable... but the world spends the money for that bread and those blankets on rockets and atomic bombs.'

'Those weapons are to defend the people, in our case.'

'Those weapons, in all cases, are to defend the cliques of ephemeral petty tyrants who enslave human beings. In the name of the people, the people are enslaved, and whenever freedom is mentioned, freedom is eradicated from the world... Please understand, I'm not talking about a "politically aware" freedom of the masses, which is no more than pure theory, a way of arranging the heap in a different way: I'm talking about that sacred, individual freedom, which sat down at the clean tables of our forefathers and was rocked in the cradles of our children. You have killed the songs of the peasants with the levelling blade of collective marches; the poetry of your youth with the official formula of a pseudo-poetry that sings of anguish and violence.'

'It is the class struggle...'

'There are no classes among human beings; you have invented them like a trampoline to jump on the heads of the desperate. There are, indeed, abnormal and unjust situations, in which man is exploited by man, but only the verticalization of everyone will enable a healthy morality to sweep away selfishness and overthrow the selfish. Shout: "Love! God! Concord!", and you will hear the hinges of history creak, and the doors of tomorrow will open before you. You found division and you have technified its jaws so that they devour the unfortunate even more quickly.'

'We have made everyone equal.'

'You have made everyone equal at the height of the lowest, by decapitating the best. You have promoted technicians, but not humanists; technicians for your machinery of war. You have created a horizontal empire that spreads like a stain of repulsive blood of a modern hydra; you have many heads, but not a single thought. You possess many regulations, but not a single piece of morality.'

'Morality is what benefits the party!'

'Party is partition, separation, struggle and ruin... The only party is that which benefits morality.'

The dialogue came to an end and the ship quickly left the protected area of the port. Before leaving the territorial waters, my captain had already ordered the letters which had until recently made up the name of my ship to be taken down. When he came to inform me of this fact, his subtle, sarcastic smile seemed to me, for the first time, welcome.

A current of sympathy circulated among all the members of my entourage, because such is the nature of human beings that when they feel a dislike for something and everyone feels it, that repulsion unites them almost as much as a shared attraction.

I returned to my cabins; I was not sad, but concerned about the immediate destiny of humanity. I thought about that door of history of which I had spoken... It does not have its hinges on one of its sides, but in the middle. If someone pushes in the centre, he will never move it; only the sides are sensitive to the pressure that will make it turn... But the movement, which is slow at first, gathers speed and, turning around completely, presents us with the unknown side, and we find ourselves on the opposite side of the same door, facing the direction in which we had been coming... Everything is so complex and yet so simple.

The knowledge of the cyclic laws consoles us, but does not help us. I felt really concerned about the immediate destiny of humanity... and I still am. Even more than about my own destiny, which at times seems to me trivial and insignificant, even if it is all I have... Or perhaps I don't even have it, because, as I am a dog, I have devoted myself entirely to humans.

But what is strange about a dog mutating into a man, if so many men have been transformed into dogs? Everything changes, and not always, at least in appearance, for the better... That too I learnt, more through my life and suffering than from the teachings of my wise master. He taught me these bitter truths in such a way that they tasted sweet to me.

CHAPTER SEVEN

# MY THIRD JOURNEY

As a complete contrast, and yet complementary to the great country I had just visited, I turned the bows of my ship towards the other colossus, the superpower that disputed the supremacy of the world with the former. I deliberately chose the longest route; I needed to meditate and be able to appreciate what I had seen, as well as to prepare myself calmly for what I was going to see. Furthermore, I really wanted to moor my ship in the harbour of the city that was considered to be one of the most populous and, of course, the most important in the world.

Travelling at half speed ahead, the crossing lasted two months. All that time I spent reading my favourite books, by classical authors. My master and teacher had taught me that, whenever the calamities of the present world overwhelmed me, I should go back to the eternal sources in search of peace and spiritual support. Thus, I re-read the *Vedas*, the *Mahâbhârata*, the *Râmâyana*, Confucius, Lao Tzu, Homer, Plato, Virgil, Plotinus, Seneca, Marcus Aurelius, the *Bible*, the *Koran*, the *Dhammapada* and many others. I read for an average of sixteen hours a day. The rest of the time, apart from what was taken up by the needs of the body, I spent listening to baroque music and the titanic Wagner. I would have liked to sculpt ivory, carve “puzzle balls” in the Chinese manner, and also paint; but my front paws never managed to fully transform into skilful hands, and only I know how difficult I found it to walk on the tips of the toes of my hind legs, sheathed in orthopaedic ankle boots.

During that period of rest, almost naked and lying on the soft rug in my bedroom, I would read tirelessly or, curling up my body, allow myself to be transported by the music, which I liked to listen to at full volume. My electronic organ awaited me in my nights of insomnia, and although my fingers had no agility, I found a way to play it reasonably well, with certain adaptations. My crew was so efficient, and my intellectuals were so occupied in their respective tasks that nothing came to disturb me. On the contrary, when I was relaxing in my bed in the human manner, I immensely enjoyed the rolling of the sea that rubbed my ear against the pillow, pulled by the inertia of my body. Only a solitary person will be able to understand me...

These profound pleasures of the spirit, or very simple ones of the body, restored peace to my soul – or the equivalent to a soul that we dogs have – and, one morning, I received a card from the captain inviting me to dine with him that night so that we could discuss the new name of the boat, since we would be arriving in port the next day. Thus, my peace and my rest came to an end, and after dinner the astute mariner handed me a piece of paper which simply said: *Capitalist Republican Democratic Order*. I don't remember being surprised by his new act of ingenuity, but I repeated my phrase that always saved me from embarrassing moments: "Let's drink to that". All the glasses were raised; we had a long and enjoyable conversation, and I went back to rest, while a group of sailors assembled the new name at the stern and the bow. Once I was in bed, I picked up the telephone and, connecting with the captain, asked him about the current name of the helicopter: "*Republic*", he told me. I hung up the receiver and fell asleep thinking about the plasticity of the human mind and its innate capacity for deception.

The next day we sailed into the enormous port, passing under a colossal bridge. As soon as we had passed it, we caught sight of the largest statue in the world. Built on a metal structure a hundred years before, it rose fifty metres above the pedestal which was about the same height again. The right arm of the statue held up an electric torch. Small vessels ploughed the waters and tugboats teemed in the distance. Two helicopters carrying reception committees had landed on my ship and, as we made our way towards the dock, a deafening choir of sirens assailed our ears, while myriads of pennants fluttered from our short masts.

Assisted by tugboats, we finally docked, and in front of us, amidst the evening fog, we saw the wonder of that colossal city, with buildings as high as mountains, whose light-filled pinnacles pointed to an endless sky.

The welcome speeches were brief, though clothed in official formulism and with some considered words on abstractions such as "freedom", "democracy" and "human rights". In reality, we all knew that freedom is not an end in itself, but a means to reach something, such as nobility and goodness, and if that something is not there, freedom becomes an instrument for exploiters and a catchphrase to silence gullible people; that democracy might have existed in a Swiss canton in the last century, where everyone knew each other and voted for an actual human being, but in modern states, made up of millions of anonymous individuals, the propaganda which is moved by vested interests can raise anyone up or bring anyone down; the people don't vote for someone they know, but for an advertising image, a smile, or for someone who is sufficiently immoral to promise them wonderful things obtained without any effort. As for human rights, everyone knew that an underworld crime boss had many more powerful influences in his favour than a humble road sweeper. But from human beings I had learned to be careful about showing my emotions or my thoughts, and friendly words closed the glittering, but false circle.

The following day, after some tumultuous interviews with journalists who literally besieged my hotel, I was able to escape with a few members of my entourage to look around the city. It was truly enormous, but very noisy, disorderly and dirty. The ethnic melting pot heated up the components of different races, but had not managed to weld them together. Puerto Ricans, Chinese, black people and Italians lived in separate neighbourhoods and their contacts with one another were more hostile than fraternal. Each group exaggerated its own characteristics to a ridiculous extent, and what was formally a cosmopolitan metropolis was at heart no more than a monstrous agglomeration of irreconcilable elements. Freedom, lacking any ideals apart from material comfort and certain rules of polite coexistence, which were not always observed, had given birth to an individual introversion which no amount of physical closeness could make up for. I have never seen so many lonely people crowded together.

When we dogs meet each other in the street, we either fight each other or love each other. The human beings in this gigantic city did neither one thing nor the other, which didn't make them better than us. At the same time, an innate atavism reconciled me with the city, because I had never seen so much love for dogs anywhere else, although that love was a way of expressing towards harmless beings an affection which no human could be found worthy of.

One afternoon we visited what at that time was the tallest building in the world. Built more than 30 years earlier, it stood more than four hundred metres high and was a truly colossal construction. From its viewing platform, which rose above the clouds of smog that shrouded the streets, the spectacle produced vertigo, because waves of mist floated past and around it, so that when one faced in their direction it was like standing on the prow of a ship, while from the other side it was like being at the stern, watching the confused wake that it left behind. The building, obviously, was not moving, but the illusion was so complete that it made me reflect on so many things that we think are motionless and yet are no more than rocks that remain upright amidst the maelstrom of movement. Backward and forward movements are, in reality, illusions produced by unmoving things. Is it the universe that is moving in the sight of the soul, or is the latter travelling through the universe? A childish question, which will make philosophers smile, but which they will not be able to answer satisfactorily. The fact is that, just as Moassy proposes a toast when he doesn't know what to say, human beings smile...

Following an invitation to make an extensive tour of that great country, I remember a few aspects that impressed me. The first thing was that there was very little connection between the big city and the rest of the country, since each region possessed its own idiosyncrasy. The people from smaller and more rationally designed cities were extremely friendly and kind, with a high standard of living and a natural inclination towards harmonious coexistence that was almost like in a village.

The problem, however, lay with the young people, who had developed an expectant apathy and a sickly admiration for all things foreign and exotic.

The moral driving forces that had transformed an undefined agglomeration of traders, bandits and trappers into the greatest power the world had seen in the last century were, if not broken, at least stagnant.

Material comfort, which had previously been a pleasant accessory, had become something indispensable; now transformed into a society of febrile consumption, the financial consortiums exploited the weaknesses of the people, and the movement of money had stifled the movement of ideas.

A suicidal cult to technification, with its statistics and its planning, had replaced the humanistic elements, and young people, though tired of all that aimless movement, had not managed to channel their dissatisfaction in any positive way, due to a lack of energy. A great lack of willpower had resulted in a spiritual laziness, and the ideas of young people stretched and contracted like big black cats on every intellectual rooftop. A certain collective guilt complex inhibited any bold enterprises and made the younger generation tend towards the overvaluation of less developed ways of life. Young people happily imitated the dress of "Simba" guerrillas or Native Americans, but would never have agreed to dress up as Greek philosophers or Roman warriors.

In the capital, the images of the great creators of this nation slept in their dreams of monumental marble, but the young people, subtly undermined by systems of subversive propaganda, tended to criticize them without mercy and to superimpose on these images – which by their fruits had proved to be good seeds – those of fashionable guerrillas who, like the women described by Schopenhauer, had long hair but were short on intelligence. The fact that those guerrillas had not been able to change the progress of the world by one iota, and that wherever those leftist ideologies had been applied, they had proved to be absolutely ineffective, did not manage to stir their drowsy souls, which only expressed themselves with feelings of dissatisfaction and nonconformism, but without proposing or providing any practical solutions.

I remember two experiences in particular which I took from the many conversations I had with people of the younger generation.

Once, in a museum of a great city in the west, I met a young person who was writing down copious details in a notebook from his study of some Attic Greek vases. I was surprised by his dedication, but even more by the fact that he was wearing, like the Native Americans, a hair band and a feather on his head. His erudition on such a classical subject did not match that devotion to the hunters of the plains. When I asked him about this, he told me that he was a lover of truth and that, as he understood that those Indians also worshipped the same, he wore an eagle's feather on his forehead to indicate his love of truth. I walked away confused; I experienced a mixed feeling of sweet hope which clashed with the harsh reality that his individual protest, though innocent and immensely valid, was at the same time absolutely impotent. That young person was the germ of a new, purer, more spontaneous humanity, which at the same time will be more respectful of the principles which are the very foundations of civilization; but, at the same time, he was the symbol of frustration, a desperate cry of loneliness in the darkness...

The other case that is recorded in my memory is of an opposite nature. In a well-kept park, I had noticed for several days a ragged young man with long hair and a shaggy beard sitting on the lawn. His appearance, in general, was that of a philosopher, a thinker. He sat motionless in the oriental lotus position known as *padmasana*. I approached and asked him what he was thinking about. He half-opened his eyes, and in a rather cruder language than was to my taste and than I am using here, he replied that he was meditating about how much his weight might be worth in human manure. Surprised, I pricked up my ears imperceptibly and, before my companions could interrupt him, I continued questioning him in the most natural way possible about why he thought such a subject was important, adding that, like natural fertiliser, the value would vary in different places around the world. He then showed me a little book where he had carefully noted down the market prices. I tried in vain to make him see that his "meditation" was stupid and pointless, and that, by imagining himself as detritus, he was identifying with a very low nature and degrading himself. His reply was painfully irrational; for him the whole of humanity was made of excrement; it was just that no one was aware of it. He felt important and courageous for expressing it and meditating about it... I left him making his absurd calculations and thought how good it would be for him to do some hard work on the land, or dig in a mine, instead of sitting there idly, cradling the monstrous creations of his circular ideas. As I was leaving, I took a last look at him; he was the very image of defeat; he remained seated, meticulously noting down the thousand faces of his fantasies in the form of excrement.

But these were exceptions, although unfortunately well publicized abroad. People lived well and were surprisingly healthy in body and soul. Some chimeras of the nineteenth century, some abstractions that had served as a spur to robust men, were now simply undermining the foundations of the most powerful state in the world. They had believed in a utopian absolute freedom, and that unnatural belief was being paid for in the bitter fruits of a general disbelief in permanent values, which was harming young people. As the other face of the materialism of contradictions, the materialism of superimpositions had failed in what is most important: the spirit of the human being.

The most extraordinary aspect of all this was that, when I pointed out these dangers in my lectures, everyone agreed, but afterwards they continued mechanically as before without taking any action to stop the rot. The horror of tyranny which they had developed as a result of the experiences of their forebears, who had fled the old continent as refugees, had precipitated them into the worst form of tyranny: the tyranny of the many.

The two superpowers I had visited one after the other were not opposites, except in their ways of life and their abstractions. On the ideological level they were more joined together than complementary. The regenerating powers of the spirit did not exist in either of them; both of them had disowned their traditions, and both of them encouraged, in different ways, the dissolution of the core elements of society. Both had combated in a thousand different ways the movements based on mysticism and tradition, and had also supported and given shelter to liberaloid leaders and factions, who hoisted the red and black flags of atheistic anarchism.

Today I think that both of them will perish together, and that perhaps neither would be able to survive without the other, unless profound changes in their structures lead those noble nations back to the natural path and free them from the tyrannies of parties, clans, consortiums and trusts, relighting the extinguished torches of their young people, with a spark ignited by the vigorous impact of the stone of ancestral traditions against the iron of an ideology which is not only new, but also better.

When I returned to the great city, I found it even more grey than before, and a timid sun, afraid of being a Sun, ashamed of its own brightness, bid farewell to the white mass of my ship which, at full speed ahead, set sail for the waters of the Atlantic.

That journey raised many questions within me, and a sense of instability took hold of me. I returned to my classics, and, as always, they gave me answers and peace.

CHAPTER EIGHT

# MY FOURTH JOURNEY

My last visit had brought about in my travelling companions a child-like, sparkling, but superficial cheerfulness. It was important that they should now see other different perspectives. The old dog who always remained beneath the appearance of Dr Moassy did not let himself be deceived by externals; we dogs often sniff something before accepting it or rejecting it, but they were humans. They had lost their atavistic instincts and had not yet replaced them with intuition; and thus, as they did not know the best, they were satisfied with the new, which tends to arrive and announce itself by name. It was evident that the systematic repetition of the word "freedom" had penetrated their consciousness, and an almost imperceptible kind of disorder was making itself felt throughout the boat.

Somewhat confused, I thought it over in my cabin, naked, with my hind quarters lying to one side, my chest on the ground and my jaw softly resting on my hands, which is the position in which we dogs place ourselves when we want to mull over some problem. I let myself remain in this state for I don't know how long.

But I do remember that the light gradually dawned in my dark dog's intelligence. The "Enigma" had made a commitment from the beginning of time to each of the innumerable creatures, and the most essential freedom was, precisely, to renounce freedom in the fraternal commitment that binds the cosmos together. From the limitation of one thing, the other is born; but the spirit passes singing from vessel to vessel, like water. The secret of the song is in that continuous and optimistic transfer, and the only notion of eternity for manifested beings is the continuation of the song and the hope of the great silence that must follow it, when all the vessels are broken. From the dust of these, new vessels will be born, and from the new vessels, new songs. Afterwards...? What can a dog know about that? But what I had understood was enough for me.

I called the captain and gave him precise orders to provide work for everyone; I gave him a new course and a new destination. That disconcerting man gave me his cold smile and said: 'I was awaiting those orders, Doctor.' After a quick bow, he moved away without ceasing to smile.

Shortly afterwards, I noticed that my companions were taking up their rhythm of work again, and I myself regained my habitual calm. But, now that so much time has passed, I confess it: whenever my eyes met those of the captain, the terrible suspicion arose that the person who could anticipate my own unexpected decisions in such a way might know my great secret. Perhaps he is the only one who will not be surprised when he reads these pages, or perhaps he will. Of the many enigmas with which I die, he is one of the greatest. Perhaps in the black hut that awaits me, I may find that answer, although my dog's instinct tells me that I will find it empty. That more than a room it will be like a bridge that will have two doors, and that I won't emerge from it very different from how I am going to enter it. If the future is the child or grandchild of the past, by the law that rules all descent, the most likely thing is that it will be similar to it. Surprise, like the hollow space in a pitcher, diminishes as the water of the assimilation of experience fills life. Philosophical surprise and wonder are so similar and antithetical that, even if Plato had not explained it through the mouth of Socrates, I would venture to do it myself. But my time in this world is ending, and I need to finish the story of my unbelievable life.

The increasingly cold wind reminded me that our southerly route was bringing us closer to a new destination. Well wrapped up, I went to the bow, where the captain was having the initials of the name of my ship placed in the necessary order. Anticipating, as always, my curiosity, he handed me some sheets where the name was written: Countryside Reform Development Operation. Sensing the futility of my question, I asked him about the current name of the helicopter, and listened to his unexpected reply:

'It's called Reform, Dr Moassy.'

Now almost sick of my own game, I turned on my hind legs and went back to my apartments, where I locked myself in so that I wouldn't have to come out until our arrival.

The current revolutionary government in power, after checking that my stay would enable it to secure further refinancing of its external debt through contact with the powerful economists who were accompanying me, radioed their welcome. The country we were going to visit was one of the many formed out of the disintegration of the former Spanish Empire in America. Since then, in one revolution after another, different "saviours of the country" had been elevated to power, alternating with periods of imitation of the great democracy of the north, which were as disastrous as the tyrannical governments called revolutionary and reformist, or even more so. During those "legalistic" lapses, chattering chambers of representatives, in spite of their ineptitude, had not been able to crush the vigorous strength of the incalculable natural riches, always well paid for by the older and more densely populated countries. In that respect, the "revolutionary" form had outdone them, because the country, potentially extremely rich, was immersed in desperate poverty, giving rise to acts of violence and revenge of all colours.

As my ship arrived, I could see that the port was well designed and built, but there seemed to be very little activity. Or rather, the activity was taking place so slowly that it seemed at first sight that there was nothing going on. In the background, the tall buildings spoke of better times, when the European wars had enabled them to sell food or fuel at the price of gold. The world peace was evidently disastrous for that community, which spent more than it produced, if its production was placed on the international market at competitive prices.

The representatives of the "Saviour of the Country" who was at that time ruling the destiny of the country received me dressed in splendid uniforms covered in so many medals that they almost hid the colour of the cloth. They were, however, pleasant people, cheerful and eager to show me their achievements. Together with the dignitaries who had welcomed me, committees of schoolchildren and diverse delegations set a tone of goodwill which - although I was not unaware that it was forced by a curious protocol - had the virtue of making me feel well disposed towards them. We dogs have always been prone to fraternize with children and humble people. But my human facade forced me to adopt the stiff postures of routine. Those accompanying me arranged an official dinner, and some unexpectedly luxurious cars took me to a hotel where the typical local touches did not quite manage to cover its totally foreign characteristics, built and serviced for tourists and carriers of currencies, for which there was so much need.

At the gala dinner, I met the leaders of that revolution, almost all of them related by family ties or interests. I found their desire to flatter me embarrassing, and often became engrossed in observing the flight of flies, a dog-like pastime which I could never quite overcome. I amused myself with the idea of what my dinner companions would think if I had surrendered to the temptation of snapping at those which came closest to my head. I think I smiled at this idea several times, but no one took it amiss, because they probably thought I was doing so because I was having a good time.

One question surprised me:

'What do you think, Doctor, of the Third World?'

I only managed to answer:

'That it is the logical continuation of the first plus the second.'

A deafening chorus of applause almost made me jump out of my seat and, reacting quickly, I decided to pay more attention to the banquet.

Thus, I discovered that a journey to the interior had been scheduled with my entourage, so that I could see the "development". It was explained to me how the revolution had caused foreign imperialism to retreat, reasserting the workers' rights and distributing the land in a vast plan of "reform", and how there were enemies of the "revolution" who were working against it with the support of stateless vested interests. Everything national was exalted and everything foreign was denigrated; but perhaps some involuntary expression on the faces of the economists who were accompanying me made them make the reservation that they were not referring to us, because they considered us "revolutionaries and reformers". I put an end to the monologue, which was becoming tense, by raising my glass and resorting to my stock phrase: "Let's drink to that!" All of us stood up and knocked back our champagne - imported, of course - and we were released.

The following days showed us a group of idealists, with good intentions but not much efficiency, fighting, on the one hand, against the agents of the superpowers who saw in the rich, impoverished and faltering country an opportunity to extend their tentacles, and also, on the other hand, fighting against the ruling group, plutocrats fond of good food, crowd-pleasing expressions and starting many projects without finishing any of them. Thus, we saw Russian machinery left to rot alongside piles of North American spare parts; Japanese locomotives that didn't fit on German rails, and Czechoslovak weapons lying next to boxes of French ammunition. Immense hospitals were almost empty, and modern schools stood out conspicuously in remote mountain areas, with no teacher in attendance. The few useless "supersonic fighter planes" thundered past above the clapped-out city buses, but, lacking adequate maintenance and having been bought third-hand, they were doomed to become scrap metal in a few months' time.

Some modern and well designed cities were surrounded by hundreds of thousands of shacks made of corrugated metal and branches. These "shanty towns" were moved periodically, amidst a great noise of propaganda, and were renamed "workers' districts" or "housing developments", always begun with cement and a marble foundation stone and "finished" with reeds and straw. In the cities, thousands of beggars; and in the fields almost no one, because the "agrarian reform" had broken up the workforce and, without an organizing head, the many arms preferred to grip a bottle of alcohol rather than the handles of a plough which, because it now belonged to everyone, no longer belonged to anyone.

I could see how human beings, like us dogs, prefer the smallest of pleasures or achievements if they can enjoy them in peace and discretion, to the most resounding but cold and subjective accomplishments lacking in warmth that are prefabricated to justify a propaganda machine, which the people always obey, but never understand; just as we dogs also obey whips, even though we never understand them. And is not propaganda, in the hands of these "revolutionaries", a great whip that drives without explaining and shames without ceasing to wound?

My subsequent conversations convinced me of the good intentions of many of these "reformers", but they also made me see the limitations to which they were subjected by a constructed autochthonous mythology, that was constantly being promoted by activists and by bandits renamed as "guerrillas". In short, everyone spoke many words, made even more plans and promoted drastic acts of violence, not only from political platforms, but even from university chairs and religious pulpits; but no one wanted to work seriously or agreed to build sources of wealth, following the old law of a cause-effort that precedes an effect-achievement, preferring fantastic demands and nationalizations of mines, land and factories, which foreigners were in a hurry to sell off because they had ceased to be productive and profitable. Thus, with a great song and dance I saw inaccessible or impoverished oilfields that had been "nationalized"; land eroded by intensive and single crop cultivation; transport systems that no international insurance company would have wanted to cover under normal policies. And while so much zeal went into giving a national colour to those imagined riches, the true wealth, which is youth, was abandoned in the hands of foreignizing activists. The result was plain to see.

A minister asked me:

'What is your opinion, Doctor, of our nationalizations? Soon we won't be importing anything...'

I didn't want to deceive him; I opened my simple dog's heart and said:

'I don't know about that... but I do know that soon you will have to import ideologists and ideologies. You robustly defend some semi-sterile or poorly cultivated fields, but you surrender the marvel of your youth, which is your future, into foreign hands. Artists, writers, philosophers, are being won over one by one by foreign doctrines and teachers. You have taught the people how to shout, but not how to work. While the civilized nations you despise have cast off their rope-soled sandals, your children go barefoot and you shod them with words, you clothe them with fantasies, you cover them with myths and promises of a future which is always future, never present... I don't apologize for my frankness, but for having been silent for so long.'

My interlocutor said nothing, but then no doubt commented on my words to one of the big shots of the "reformist government", because a few days later I was very politely invited to bid farewell to them and continue my onward journey.

And so I left them with their dreams, with their future without a present, with their past without a present. And to the displeasure of my human economic advisers, who had seen the opportunity of some good business based on numbered accounts, I gave the order to leave immediately. My ship set sail by night and in silence, like an opportunity which is slipping away.

Once we were on the high seas, I had to put up with the bitter criticisms of my travelling companions, who accused me of a lack of diplomatic tact. I had to remind them that I was paying them too well for them to try to take advantage of my travels to further exploit nations that were already being cheated. Then I consoled myself alone, considering that we dogs may not have a quick intelligence, but that our simple heart more than made up for it.

I was startled by a remark from my captain:

'Doctor,' he said, 'forgive me if I tell you that your reaction was not entirely human...'

And my uneasiness was not due to his words alone, but to his sarcastic smile.

CHAPTER NINE

# MY FIFTH JOURNEY

The recent disagreements had separated me psychologically from my human crew and I remember the strange sensation of dejection against which I had to fight for a long time. I believe that what distanced me from my companions in adventure was not exactly the fact that I was a dog, but that, by dint of pretending to be human, that mask had become so embedded in me that it gave rise to a struggle within myself. My placid and contemplative nature had left me, and no sooner had I picked up a book than I exchanged it for another. Scarcely had I sat down at my electronic organ, than it occurred to me to rearrange the display cases of the museum, or to do some target practice with a pistol on deck. I imagine that human beings feel like that generally and that is the root of their apparent contradictions, which are contradictions if we don't compare them or superimpose them. Each moment has its value, its attraction and its repulsion, and the next moment can be as dissimilar to it as the dark night that follows the brightest of days.

Thus, I gave the captain an uncertain course, with the excuse that it would enable my scientists to collect samples of marine fauna and flora; meanwhile, I waited for time to bring about my dehumanization.

I remembered a teaching I had learned from a question I had asked an ophthalmologist some time ago. My wise master had taught me to gather little nuggets of wisdom even from the most ordinary and sterile sands. The above-mentioned professional, to whom I had gone to seek treatment for some little spots that were floating in the liquid of my eye and appeared as little dots wherever I fixed my gaze, gave me the following advice:

'Doctor, try not to pay attention to them and look directly at what you want to see; if you withdraw your attention from them, you won't see them.'

And indeed, I didn't see them again, except when I remembered them.

So, from that time onwards, I busied myself with the most routine tasks, my always plentiful correspondence, walking on deck and observing the flight of the cormorants, and not worrying about anything else. I forgot for the moment the purpose of my journeys and my own quest. I also forgot about my entourage and I left the efficient captain in charge of everything.

As the weeks passed, my inner dog began to resurface. Expecting nothing from the future, I lived in the present moment fully and calmly. I regained my good humour and my simple habits. I was able to immerse myself again in my books and spend long and uncounted hours playing my organ. And in the solitude of my rooms, I lay flat on the floor and snuffled placidly without knowing what day or time it was. I ate when I was hungry and slept if my eyelids became heavy, not caring whether the sun was high in the sky or whether the bracelets of the stars were glittering above my ship.

In the midst of that freedom, I rediscovered the obedience to my destiny. Only then did I go up to the bridge and ask the officer on deck to summon the captain. Always smiling and dapper, he entered silently, and sitting next to me in front of the control panel, he joined me in contemplating the raging sea, whose wet hair lashed against the circular windows, which were transparent and clean due to the movement of the sea. After a time - I no longer remember how long - he asked me if I thought that the teams of scientists had found what they were looking for. After absent-mindedly leafing through the thick folder of reports, I walked over to the chart table, and gave him as our course a route that led to the African continent. Without further comment, he gave the necessary orders and both of us watched the greenish eye on the radar screen with fascination. A storm had been unleashed with great fury, and after I had told him the port I wanted to arrive at and informed him of my intention to fly by helicopter to one of the small new central republics, I withdrew, walking with difficulty due to the frightful rolling of the ship.

As soon as I was back in my rooms, the internal telephone brought me the calm, metallic voice of that imperturbable man:

'Do you agree to your ship now being called Downtrodden Race Of Colour?'

'Yes,' I replied. 'But what will the helicopter be called?'

After a short silence, he answered, for once:

'Could you give me a little more time? I don't know yet.'

I hung up the receiver and laughed long and hard. At last, my omniscient captain had not been able to give me an answer. I believe that this was the little thing I needed to regain my natural cheerfulness. Humans had infected me with the diabolical virtue of celebrating any failure on the part of others. When I realized this, the next day I sought out the captain and, patting him affectionately, told him that, in view of the bad weather, I didn't want the helicopter to be taken out of the hold until the storm had abated and that I would give the order. That cold man, who was worried about not being able to fulfil his part of the game for the moment, shot me a look of gratitude. Then I realized that he, too, was sensitive, and I tried never to forget it. The fact is that I didn't always remember that humans wore masks of rigidity to hide a more tender interior. So of course, my captain couldn't be an exception, although he seemed to be.

Once the storm had passed, I called the captain and ordered

the two helicopters to be taken out of the hold; my personal one had the word *Racism* written on its flank. Surprised, I pointed out that such a name might seem offensive to those who, precisely, were fighting to overcome differences of skin colour. After smiling enigmatically, the captain assured me that it would not give a bad impression and, before I had time for any further questions, that singular man disappeared from my sight with his eternal smile on his lips. The future would prove him right. My instinct – I acknowledge it – was not always as accurate as his cunning. Perhaps I never completely managed to understand human beings.

I remember that I found our entry into the port particularly enjoyable, because the tropical beauty was combined with the typical colourfulness of the people's costumes, alongside the modern and well equipped facilities. But I was not so interested in the country that welcomed me at that moment, because it was governed by an administration of a European type, so it didn't allow me to appreciate, in its appropriate setting, the characteristics of a new country formed by people of colour. Consequently, after the brief welcome speeches and the delight of the white men about the name of the helicopter and that of the black men about the name of my boat, without any apparent conflict – since the ideological was submerged in that place by the economic – I boarded my helicopter with a dozen of my fellow travellers, while the other helicopter carried delegates from the nation we were about to visit.

I believe that the speed with which we disembarked and then took off again prevented any hostile comments. Sometimes velocity not only overcomes balance, as the well-known law of the mechanics of bodies states, but also triumphs over imbalance, at least on the psychological level. There I learnt that, in order to be well received by everyone, there is nothing better than to leave immediately.

From the air I could see that the image of progress and civilization offered by the coastal area was immediately replaced by thick virgin vegetation and wretched shanty towns. We also flew over arid zones of rocky ground, where huts and tents stood in close proximity to surprisingly small green areas. As they watched us fly past, the locals down below waved joyfully and, in order to leave them with a happy memory, we dropped some boxes of food and medicine by parachute. As my helicopters had a long range, we were able to reach the capital we had chosen in a single flight. From above, it looked small, well laid out in the centre, but surrounded by miserable-looking shanty towns. I was surprised, however, by the happiness with which the people rushed to meet us when we landed. I soon realized that they were motivated more by their expectation of our gifts than what they might learn about us. But their attitude was more childlike than materialistic, and from what I could see later, completely lacking in malice. Like us dogs, they were people accustomed to running, either out of happiness or fear. I was able to understand that more easily than my very cultured human companions who shared the experience.

The reception committee was attired with a strange mixture of indigenous elements, European medals, American shirts and Russian weapons. But they were all smiling. The speeches singled out the name of my ship, although they didn't mention that of my helicopter.

Several days later, in a comfortable bungalow, I was received by the senior officials of the tiny state. My complexion, which had never become completely fair, must have inspired them with great trust, because they behaved in an exceptionally friendly way towards me. They spoke to me for a long time about their struggles for liberation from the whites, whom they considered little short of demons. They congratulated me once again about the name of my boat and, to my surprise, that of my helicopter as well. Without turning round, I could feel the cynical smile of my captain who, sitting a few metres behind me with the rest of the entourage, kept himself at a prudent distance.

They explained to me that, now that the internal situation had been dealt with by the deportation of all the white residents, they had to face the world around them. Their mines of diamonds and rare metals would enable them to negotiate further progress. But what really caught my attention was that, far from being inclined towards a human understanding beyond the colour of a person's skin, these people were actually dreaming of revenge.

For them, now that the myth of white supremacy had been discarded, that of black supremacy should prevail. Arguments about the demographic growth of people of colour in the Western countries alternated with other pseudo-scientific arguments about the antiquity of the black race, combined with the geological discoveries that had found – at least so they believed – that the early Europeans had been black and that the most ancient fossil man was also black. Finally, I was led to understand that white, yellow and red people were no more than impermanent mutations of an ancestral black race that possessed the genetic keys to the future. They prophesied the total extermination of all those who were not black. Then I learnt that the word *Racism*, now that it was in the possession of their state, had changed its content. Anti-racism had been the flag brandished against the whites and should continue to be raised in other parts of the globe; but there, a "constructive" racism was necessary to reserve for black people all the key posts and powers of government. This was explained again and again at great length, not only as a means of defence against the white oppressor, but – and this was the fundamental and almost esoteric part of their theory, suitable only for its initiates – as an instrument of a "black power" that had to be reintroduced all over the world. Memories of the slave raids were mixed over and over again with statistics of genetic and psychological testing, seasoning everything with anthropological and archaeological "confidential reports".

I didn't dare to contradict them. Like children with a new toy, they were discussing all this, which might be the seed of some future genocide, without ceasing to smile. For them the matter was so simple that it made them laugh.

I tried to point out to them that the hurried and violent exodus of white people, even those who didn't consider skin colour as a symbol of status, such as missionaries and doctors, had proved disastrous for the small nation, where the tse-tse fly, for example, had regained areas it had already abandoned in the times of Queen Victoria, in the nineteenth century; and that, at a time when they could not do without the whites, they had sent away those well-intentioned people and were now obliged to hire mercenaries who were attracted purely by self-interest and would leave the country as soon as they had completed their contracts.

I don't know whether it was because of the gentle way in which I outlined these arguments, which I have here summed up crudely, or simply because my words were going in one ear and out the other, that they cheerfully explained to me that all these things would be sorted out very quickly, and that they didn't want white people staying for a long time in their territories because living together with them brought diseases and vices. I suggested that a strong and superior race could not be a fragile object in the hands of those carriers; and I could not avoid a little sarcasm. This had no effect either on my friendly interlocutors, who argued once again that they were only momentarily weak and permeable as a result of having lived together for so long with the white man.

After that, one argument followed another. Those people were tireless in their conversations and almost everything was celebrated with great roars of laughter. In the early hours of the morning, I told them I would not like to leave without visiting some towns in the interior, but, smiling all the time, they refused me permission on the grounds there were white guerrillas in those areas, which made them dangerous.

'But there are also dark-skinned guerrillas who plant bombs in European airports!' I exclaimed, losing my patience with such stubborn narrow-mindedness.

Far from getting angry, they burst out laughing, explaining how those people did it because they were paid by white interests, and that this was self-evident, since no black people ever planted bombs in their own airports. I couldn't help being startled by the platitude, but soon a religious service was organized, a mixture of Protestant Christianity and African rituals, and they all accompanied me singing to the hotel. Inexplicably, they clearly liked me very much and – I confess – I wished them, when leaving, with all my heart, the best of luck; although rationally I knew that the routes they had chosen were heading towards enormous pools of blood which, whether of black or white people, is always red.

I remember that on the return journey, I avoided all discussion with the members of my entourage and maintained a gloomy silence for a long time. I didn't want to hear the opinions of my companions, because I sensed that they would be of an opposite nature to those we had heard, but of similar fanaticism and stupidity, which, although more erudite, is fanaticism and stupidity all the same.

Once again, I set some oceanographic tasks for my ship, and remained in my rooms for more than a month, naked and curled up, with my eyes half closed, barely eating, and sleeping all day. That is the position by which we dogs indicate that we are bored; and I was already bored of human beings.

Today I would like to believe in that fable of Ovid which says that animals have a different paradise from that of humans.

And yet I know that, without their voices, I would feel terribly alone. Even in these moments, when the muffled sounds of their voices reach me through the thick walls of my study, my ears imperceptibly prick up and I wag my non-existent tail. And the fact is that, although I was never able to understand them, I have never ceased to love them. In truth, for dogs the fundamental thing is not intellect, but love. And we love humans unrelentingly.

Try it yourself, reader; cross the path of the most unknown of dogs on the street and you will see how he celebrates the encounter as if you were an old friend. He doesn't understand you, but he loves you. Could you say the same of any human being? Perhaps you could... In that case, don't squander your good fortune.

But time is snapping at my hind legs and urging me to continue with this story; it is forcing me to hurry up and keep going and, in a disordered heap, to offer you my treasure of experiences. It is the treasure of a dog... they are only the bones of things that have passed... Accept them as they are, bare and dry. It is all that I could save and I am taking them out by digging in the turned-over earth of my memories. When my holes are empty, I will leave; have patience with me.

CHAPTER TEN

# MY SIXTH JOURNEY

When I called my captain and gave him a course for the East, I noted that his smile became more marked. He was not unaware that my supposed family had had close links with that part of the world, or that the Eastern classics were my favourite readings.

But my journey was not now to the past, but to the present. The strange phenomenon of the survival of extremely ancient forms of culture and the mutual exchanges they had with the surrounding world, was a new experience for me, which I had dreamt about for a long time and vaguely feared. That professional, who had spent his whole life at sea, would not find any surprises wherever I might take him, but my standpoint was different from his, and everyone has to have their own experience. So it was, that without further consultation, I told him to head for a port in South Asia, and recommended that he should prepare the helicopters for long flights across the interior. That night, as I stood on my own looking up at the stars, I saw that we were already heading north-east. A silent shadow at my back made me turn round and I found the captain standing there.

'Doctor, I have a new name for the ship; I would like to know if you approve of it,' he said.

At my gesture of assent, he ordered the lights of the poop deck to be turned on and handed me the draft documentation.

I read: *Renewed Course Of Destiny*. It sounded good to me, but before he walked away, I asked him about the name of the helicopter. This time he had no doubts and, in a quieter tone than usual, said: *Rama*. I could not conceal my astonishment, because the name of the old god of the *Ramayana* was something I would never have expected to hear from his lips. Evidently enjoying my momentary confusion, he stressed:

'And I hope you don't think I have been spying on the books in your library; I also have a fairly well stocked one of my own. It's a pity there's no longer a Hanuman to tear open his chest and reveal the ancient name of Rama on his heart, isn't it?'

After hearing this, although I recovered my composure externally, my inner doubts about that very strange human being became very great indeed. Because such a knowledge of old and exotic religions was not to be expected from his cynicism and his closely guarded – not to say tragic – superficiality and nihilism. I no longer remember what other words we exchanged, but a strange sensation, like being in the presence of the unknown, was added to the other feelings which the most senior officer on my boat inspired in me.

The port at which we arrived was congested with ships. It was evident that the enormous population of that subcontinent needed a very lively trade, and that there were not many maritime points of entry.

At the time of my journey, the destiny of that country was in the hands of a woman, and I couldn't help smiling when I remembered that one of the oldest books of that nation relegated the feminine sex to the most humble of places in all earthly matters, although, with regard to the divine, the mother goddesses were of the greatest antiquity. It was palpable that, although in the eyes of foreigners, tradition and present continued to be firmly linked together and this may also have been the case on the popular level, in official and political spheres they had become divorced in more than one respect.

This feature was the one most highlighted by the reception committee that welcomed me, but they never managed to convince me that it was something that would propel them towards the future. I found in all the public officials a strange mixture of love for their own past and a rejection of it; a wish to save the spirit while despising the forms, without considering that these had also been beautiful and efficient. And I am not referring to the priority of one sex over another, or their equivalence, but to matters of greater importance. That dichotomy, that not daring to vitalize tradition in all its possible totality and wanting to show me in the first place, at the high-level meetings I attended, the technological advances they had made, which were, on the other hand, of only minor importance, was somewhat annoying. They seemed not to know or to forget for the moment that I came from a highly technified world with a developed economy and that neither I nor those who accompanied me could be at all impressed by modern facilities, which were, on the other hand, mere islets in a sea of millions of famished and wretched beings. I shook off those carbon copies of the West as soon as possible and, with a small entourage, began to travel to different cities and to get to know all sorts of people.

The first thing that startled my dog's instinct was seeing how, in a country in which, in most of its provinces, the life of animals was totally respected, at the same time they were held in very scant regard. They were not killed, but there were not many people who cared about how they lived. You shouldn't think of that great country as if it were a whole, but as an almost feudal mosaic with different customs and beliefs; but as regards animals – even those considered sacred in several places – they were decorated and perfumed with incense more than they were looked after. Everywhere I saw myriads of bony animals trotting continuously in search of food. A common denominator of hunger united all living beings and, apart from trees and merchants, I didn't see anything strong and healthy in thousands of kilometres. The desperate monkeys of the temples, for example, picked at the always numerous but diminutive offerings that were left for them by the faithful. But as my fellow dogs were not deified by any southern sect, and as they didn't receive any affection from those people who respected everything but didn't seem to want to take any trouble over anything, they wandered about, their bodies constantly malnourished and their skin covered in sores, waiting for the death of the weaker ones so that they could be devoured by the others. In the West, I have seen the unconsciousness of the hunter who kills the innocent creatures of the countryside for sport and, at the same time, cares in an exaggerated way for his domestic animals; I was never able to understand it. But nor was I able to understand the fact that in this part of the world it was considered a crime to kill an animal, but not to leave it abandoned to its diseases and to a promiscuity that was painful to witness for anyone with the slightest sensibility.

But this phenomenon also extended to human beings. Except in the westernized communities, there was no crime, but there was no welfare either, and people would watch an old person die of fever with the same indifference with which they would watch the movement of worms, although with less curiosity.

Everything, in this nation, was due to its religious sense. The good and the bad. An excess of external rituals had enabled people to bear the inclemencies of destiny and overcome adverse conditions thanks to an incredible spiritual strength; but it had also dried them up in terms of charity and any rise in the standard of living. On seeing the long caravans of hungry devotees, the question arose as to whether it was hunger that motivated their religious processions, or religion, whose precepts forced them to abandon earthly possessions. The most likely answer, if we look at it in the light of the situation of Europe at the time of the first Crusades, which has been well studied, is that both tendencies were merged together in a powerful collective subconscious. This nation lived in a perpetual "crusade" of multiple "Jerusalems". And, as in central Europe in the eleventh century, greatness and smallness walked arm in arm; heroism and pillage; chastity and sensuality; drug addicts and sages; truly enlightened beings and conjurers: everything was mixed together without ever being completed or excluded. A contradiction without vitality, and yet with a surprising sense of perpetuity and continuity.

In any case, the scholars in my entourage who were expecting it to be relatively easy to meet people who could teach them about the ancient philosophies and religions were disappointed. And not because such people didn't exist, but because they were so mixed up with fanatics and ignorant people, that – I confess to this trait of malice in myself – I couldn't help finding their searches amusing. Behind the skeletal old man pierced by thorns and sitting among hundreds of clay cobras which his devotees had deposited at his feet, they found only a mentally impaired person. And yet they passed by without noticing the shop of a dentist who, apart from his work, was an expert translator and interpreter of the ancient texts, endowed with parapsychological powers and exemplary spiritual elevations. But these genuinely wise people – the minority, unfortunately – did not publicize themselves as such or use pompous-sounding names, like those favoured by the different "gurus" who became popular in the West. They withdrew in secret, at certain periods of their lives, to distant monasteries, and were in appearance the most ordinary people and the ones least interested in metaphysics. As the days passed, I began to distinguish two currents which, although apparently parallel and even identical, had almost no connection with one another. One, consisting of survivals of the ancient Mysteries, the guardian of secrets, about which, precisely because they are secret, all comments are untrue. And another, comprising a highly complex, colourful, hereditary and fanatical folklore, based more on external postures than on any real spiritual elevation. Vitiated by mechanical formulas and inertia, it added the word "holy" to everything and upheld a polytheism typical of all rustic and poverty-stricken populations, of all countries and times. Peasant holy men walk on burning coals in America, Africa and Asia, but at the bottom of their souls they tend to be as atheistic and amoral as any Marxist academic. They have preserved the secret of the application of a psychological technique – more of an "exaltation" than a technique – but what in the beginning was merely a means of propaganda, today is an end in itself. In these people, the secondary has usurped the place of the essential.

Seeing them, I remembered a parable recorded by Annie Besant in one of her books: *the Brahmin, the post and the cat*. The story tells of how, in some far-off time, a wise Brahmin, learned in high magic, one day found that his ceremonial table, which had been laboriously prepared, had been upset by the playing of his cat. Ever since then, whenever he was going to officiate at a ceremony, he tied the little animal to a post which he stuck into the ground at the door of the temple. After his death, his disciples, who had seen him doing this, believing it to be part of the ritual, never performed the ceremony without tying a cat to a post. With the passing of centuries, as the priesthood was difficult and required a very special training, its fundamental requirements gradually became lost, but the distant disciples of that Brahmin continued tying a cat to a post before each ceremony. When everything esoteric and difficult had been lost, the only religious expression that remained was to tie up a cat at the gates of the temple.

In short, not every secret consists of knowledge, but often of ignorance; and what is not spoken is very often not due to any esoteric reasons, but for the very simple reason that there is nothing to say. There is certainly an abyss between the reasonings of the Buddha in his disregard for the mind, and those of most of the modern "gurus". The former had overcome it; the latter deny it simply because they have not managed to develop it, or they have ended up in a dead-end and do not dare to admit it to themselves, let alone to others. There is a great distance between the king who becomes a beggar and the beggar who cannot help being one; the one renounces, the other accepts. In the first there is an act of will; in the second, of defeat.

I remember these and many other reflections blossoming in me the first time I travelled to the East. My wise master had told me the way to follow there, and God knows that I found what I was looking for; but hippies and tourists do not tend to go beyond the aspect of folklore, and unfortunately that folklore, which is so photogenic, has turned that ancient country into a vast conglomerate of hungry people and fanatics who wander among the ruins of its marvellous temples, having lost the ancient spiritual, psychological and physical strength that once transformed it into the scene of a battlefield through one of the greatest religious and philosophical works of all times, the *Bhagavad-Gita*, whose principal heroes rode in war chariots. But the age-old Kriya (War) is imagined today as the opposition between the air that comes out of the left nostril and that which comes out of the right. There were other stronger winds blowing the ancient glories, that made history and launched religions, arts and sciences around the world. Weakness is not a rejection of strength, but the lack of it. This is a very ancient teaching.

Full of mystical enthusiasm, or at least what a dog can feel in that respect, in other words, a mixture of love for my master, warmth of the sun and nibbles of grass, I departed from the old country. As a heterogeneous musical band bid farewell to our ship, I recalled the unique treasures of art, philosophy and religion that I had seen, and I dropped into the sea a thick wad of leaflets that I had been given, showing a rather more photographed than actually impressive factory of fighter planes that reproduced, of course, an out of date supersonic Russian model. I did keep a garland of flowers and leaves on which the swastikas of Vishnu and Shiva had been painted, complementing each other like the past and the future; like the flower, a memory and a promise of fruit.

CHAPTER ELEVEN

# MY SEVENTH JOURNEY

What I have entitled my seventh journey is different from the others.

What I have been trying to do is to recall the first impressions that some of the countries in the world made on me, and what their inhabitants inspired in me. After these journeys, I made many others, some to the same places, others to different parts of the planet. I spent many years giving classes and lectures, attending congresses and advising ministries. I received many honours and awards. I suffered a lot; I failed in several things; and I met on my path some excellent travelling companions, as well as some traitors.

It would be pointless to tell the whole story of my life, both for my readers and for myself. I told you at the beginning that the two infinities had always attracted me and that I had always felt lost in this horizontal world. And one who is lost can hardly recommend paths to others.

But the journey to which I am referring is not on the level of the ground, but at the extremes of that vertical axis that has always attracted me and is the one that absorbs me now. Although I also recognize that such verticality is always seen from our own horizon.

There are no parallel dimensions, only tangential ones. From separation comes union, and from union new separations arise... And so it always is. Dead leaves serve to feed the roots and, from their sacrifice, new leaves are made. Often, when running down the sides of a hill, I have suffered the illusion that the horizontal valley was rising up to meet me. It is difficult, in what is essential – which in the words of the delightful character of Saint-Exupéry's *The Little Prince*, is always invisible – to achieve that unfailing discernment of the bubble of air trapped in the liquid of a spirit level. Or that of water in a vessel which, even though we may move it, always retains the equanimity of its surface. Or that of fire which, when the burnt log is turned over, still knows where the sky is. Fire and water are two seekers of verticality, in its two directions. Air and earth seek their perpendicular horizontality. Fire over Air; Water over Earth; these are the two generative crosses of which our old treatises of alchemy tell us. When Fire passes through Air, and when Water penetrates Earth, there is generation, there is evolution, there is Time and there is Being, as we understand it. When Earth rises vertically above Water, and when Air ascends with Fire, we enter the tangential turning point of a different dimension, and then even we dogs become philosophers.

Sitting with my head tilted slightly to the side and my gaze turned upwards, I have seen the glittering bodies which capture the souls of the stars, and I have felt infinitely small, while at the same time feeling associated, in a mysterious way, with that gigantic splendour.

I have travelled a lot in my imagination, in a ship which is not re-named at every port, because it always has the same name; in an intangible helicopter which, in addition to having a perpetual initial, does not need to add moveable name-tags to itself in order to travel and be understood. When I travelled, I did so without wanting to be understood or to understand; I travelled just with the desire to travel. The sum of memories of the point forms the first line of our consciousness, and our re-encounter with places that we passed through in former times closes for us the geometric figures that capture life, but do so only in order to feel the ineffable pleasure of releasing it again and again. Draw a circumference with your finger on the beach; the sand it encloses is the same as that which surrounds it... To what extent have you changed Nature or contained it? The bottom of the furrow which your finger has traced is also made of sand and, if you observe it well, you will see that it does not exist.

As the dog that I am, I spent my life innocently observing Nature. My mental garments are alien to me and only clothe my simple will. But it is the vocation of dogs to walk naked; I have always found clothes uncomfortable, even though I recognized that they were necessary for horizontal life.

Someone who has never worn clothes will never know what it is to take them off, and this distinguishes me from other dogs. One can only abandon and free oneself from something that one once had. The beginning and the end are joined together, but the innumerable stages in between belong to another dimension, to the curved dimension of missed encounters and solitude. If you believe that the Egyptians represented Anubis with a human body and a dog's head for purely totemic reasons, you know nothing about it. Look at his feet, always in a position of walking, of travelling, and you will understand. Then let go of the understanding.

I feel that my ears are drooping, my eyes are half closing and my tiredness is turning into peace. I can no longer feel the keyboard of the typewriter under my fingers, and a very distant voice, which I recognize as that of my master, is calling me from somewhere.

Will there be other paths? I'm sure there will, but for now let me rest. I no longer have any curiosity about the black hut which is growing larger and larger in front of me. So many houses, so many things, so many landscapes, so many faces were new to me and at one time I treated them as old acquaintances... Any strange thing that may come will soon become familiar and close. It has happened to me so many times and will happen to me so many times again...!

What a great dream!

When a dog falls asleep in front of you, when everything you have loved falls asleep in front of you, let it sleep. With our eyes closed we make the best journeys. I ask you to love dogs a lot, to love all beings, and even yourselves. Don't torture yourselves constantly and have pity for the Dream which is growing inside you. It is the nostalgia for that Great Journey, the one we make with our eyes closed.

I am going to my black hut, to lie at the feet of my master. But I know that I will sleep and that comforts me. I will lick his feet before going to sleep. I am a dog; there is nothing stronger than the love for my master, and nothing sweeter than to make myself very small and curl up beside him.

I will make my seventh journey with my eyes closed. With our eyes closed we make the best journeys.

*This work was completed in Centenillo, Sierra Morena, Spain, on 20$^{th}$ May 1974.*

# ABOUT THE AUTHOR

Born in Argentina in 1930, Jorge A. Livraga Rizzi graduated from the University of Buenos Aires with a degree in History and History of Art. In 1951 he was awarded the National Poetry Prize in Argentina and, over the course of his life, was the author of poems, novels and works on philosophy, history and esoteric subjects. In 1976 he was awarded the Cross of Paris in Arts, Sciences and Literature for his services to culture. His publications include: Ankor: The Last Prince of Atlantis, The Elemental Spirits of Nature, Thebes, The Mystery Theatre in Greece: Tragedy, and several others. In 1957 he founded the "School of Philosophy in the Classical Tradition" which later became incorporated under the name of International Organization New Acropolis.

## INTERNATIONAL ORGANIZATION NEW ACROPOLIS

NEW ACROPOLIS

New Acropolis is a worldwide non-profit organization, with centres in over fifty countries.

Established by Professor Jorge Angel Livraga on the foundations of practical philosophy and universal fraternity, New Acropolis is inspired by a fundamental respect for human dignity beyond differences of race, gender, culture, religion or socio-economic status. New Acropolis respects diversity but also tries to transcend it in search of a higher unity through shared universal ethical principles.

At New Acropolis, philosophy is more than just intellectual food for thought. We study philosophy as a means to integrate science, arts, ethics and metaphysics in order to work towards global human development.

This vision is implemented through a wide range of programs that combine practical education with cultural and volunteering activities. New Acropolis also promotes an awareness of current affairs, both locally and globally and focuses on improving the human condition by aligning ourselves with the laws of nature.

To learn more about New Acropolis, visit www.acropolis.org